Ballots and Bullets

Ballots and Bullets

THE ELUSIVE DEMOCRATIC PEACE

Joanne Gowa

PRINCETON UNIVERSITY PRESS

PRINCETON, NEW JERSEY

5/00

Copyright © 1999 by Princeton University Press
Published by Princeton University Press, 41 William Street,
Princeton, New Jersey 08540
In the United Kingdom: Princeton University Press, Chichester, West Sussex

Library of Congress Cataloging-in-Publication Data

Gowa, Joanne S.
Ballots and bullets : the elusive democratic peace / Joanne Gowa.
p. cm.
Includes bibliographical references (p.   ) and index.
ISBN 0-691-00256-8 (cloth : alk. paper)
1. Peace.   2. Democracy.   3. United States—Foreign relations—1993–   I. Title.
JZ5560.G69 1999
327.1'01—dc21
98-37331
CIP

Published under the auspices of
the Center of International Studies

This book has been composed in Galliard

Princeton University Press books are
printed on acid-free paper and meet the guidelines
for permanence and durability of the Committee
on Production Guidelines for Book Longevity
of the Council on Library Resources

http://pup.princeton.edu

Printed in the United States of America

1   2   3   4   5   6   7   8   9   10

TO KATIE, JON, AND TIM

Contents

List of Figures and Tables

FIGURE

TABLES

Acknowledgments

I NEVER WOULD have begun the work that evolved into this book had it not been for Miles Kahler, the Social Science Research Council, and the University of California, San Diego. On a very cold and gray day in Philadelphia seven years ago, Miles called to ask if I wanted to participate in an SSRC-sponsored conference on liberalization and foreign policy at UCSD. In a split second, I agreed, as the vision of San Diego in March overwhelmed my reluctance to write papers for conferences.

The agenda for the conference sparked my interest in the rapidly growing democratic-peace literature. In the paper I wrote for the March meeting, I examined existing explanations of the democratic peace and found them less than compelling. However, I knew that a serious challenge to the democratic-peace hypothesis required a reanalysis of the existing data.

I turned for help to Henry Farber, a Princeton labor economist with an enduring interest in dispute-resolution processes. Hank has a command of econometric methods and an understanding of data and their limits for which I have acquired a deep respect. Fortunately, he also had the capacity to persist, with his good humor mostly intact, through the series of torturous changes that a parade of reviewers demanded. I could not have produced this book without his help.

I am also grateful to the colleagues and friends who read the entire manuscript and offered very useful, if markedly diverse, suggestions about revising it. James E. Alt, Steve Chan, Gary King, Robert G. Gilpin Jr., Robert O. Keohane, Edward D. Mansfield, Peter J. Katzenstein, and Stephen M. Walt all contributed generous amounts of their talent and time to help make the final version of the manuscript clearer and more complete than earlier drafts.

Individual chapters also benefited from the careful attention of other scholars. Among the latter, I owe more than I can gracefully express to my current and former colleagues in the politics and economics departments at Princeton, who attended what seemed even to me to be an infinite series of seminars on various aspects of the democratic peace. Anne C. Case, Larry M. Bartels, George W. Downs, Mark Fey, Gene Grossman, Keisuke Iida, Peter Kenen, John Londregan, Christina H. Paxson, Thomas Romer, and Howard Rosenthal were indefatigable sources of help. I also received very sound advice on different parts of the manuscript from Robert J. Art, Benjamin J. Cohen, Kurt Gaubatz, Peter Gourevitch, Miles Kahler, David Lake, Lisa Martin, James D. Morrow, Walter Mattli, John S. Odell, Sharyn O'Halloran, Robert Powell, Dan Reiter, Bruce M. Russett, and Randolph M. Siverson.

Malcolm Litchfield, the political science editor at Princeton University Press, never once flinched, at least observably, when I missed more than one deadline. Nor did Edna Lloyd cringe when I asked her to check the citations against the references for the first, second, or twelfth time. In a flash, Alan Krueger came up with the title for the book. Jacqueline Berger, Deborah Garvey, and Matthias Kaelberer all provided invaluable research assistance. The Center of International Studies and the Committee on Research in the Humanities and Social Sciences of Princeton University provided financial support for this project, as did a grant for Research and Writing from the John D. and Catherine T. MacArthur Foundation.

Some material from previously published papers appears in this book. I am grateful to the University of Texas Press for permission to reprint parts of "Common Interests or Common Polities? Reinterpreting the Democratic Peace" (coauthored with Henry Farber), *Journal of Politics* (vol. 59, no. 2, pp. 393–417). I also appreciate the permission of the MIT Press to use parts of three papers: "Democratic States and International Disputes," *International Organization* (vol. 49, no. 3); "Politics at the Water's Edge," *International Organization* (vol. 52, no. 2); and "Polities and Peace" (coauthored with Henry Farber), *International Security* (vol. 20, no. 2).

I dedicate this book to my children: Katie, who, from the time she was old enough to sit still, listened patiently as I practiced presenting papers, including those that led to this book; Jon, an always cheerful, willing, and invaluable source of technical support; and Timmy, a computer-literate ten-year-old with an extraordinary capacity to empathize with a recipient of bad reviews.

Joanne Gowa
March 20, 1998

Ballots and Bullets

Introduction

As a replacement for the Cold War strategy of containment, the Clinton administration has adopted a foreign-policy strategy designed to enlarge the "community of democratic nations."[1] This strategy, it maintains, "serves all of America's strategic interests—from promoting prosperity at home to checking global threats abroad" (1996, 32). It does so, according to President Clinton, because "democracies rarely wage war on one another" (1993, 3).

The administration's action finds a sympathetic echo, if not a raison d'être, in much of the recent international relations literature. Based upon multifaceted theoretical foundations and systematic empirical analyses, a series of studies concludes that democratic states are much less likely to engage each other in serious conflicts than are other states.

More specifically, these studies find, democratic states do not wage war against other democratic states. Most students of what has become known as the "democratic peace" also agree that democratic states are much less likely than are other states to engage each other in serious disputes that involve recourse to force short of war. The number of studies that supports these findings has led Jack Levy to observe, and many others to concur, that the democratic peace is "as close as anything we have to an empirical law in international relations" (1989, 270).

In this book, I reexamine both the analytic and empirical foundations of the democratic-peace hypothesis. I find that a democratic peace exists only during the Cold War. No evidence of a democratic peace is apparent before World War I. I conclude that an explanation based on shifting interests is more consistent with this dispute-rate pattern than is an explanation based on common polities. Thus, for example, the advent of relative peace between democratic states after 1945 can be interpreted as a product of the interest patterns that the advent of the Cold War induced.

This suggests that the logic and evidence that support a foreign-policy strategy of enlargement are based on a unique and now extinct era in world politics. There is no reason to believe that the democratic peace

---

[1] The effort to promote democracy abroad is one of three goals of the newly declared U.S. strategy. The others are to "bolster America's economic revitalization" and to ensure that U.S. military strength is adequate to protect U.S. security (Clinton 1996, i).

that prevailed after the Second World War will survive the erosion of the East-West split that defined the post-1945 world. This implies, in turn, that the United States might be better off if it reverted to a strategy of "building bridges" abroad; that is, an effort to construct common strategic and economic interests between nations seems likely to yield higher returns than does an effort to construct democratic regimes within nations. However desirable it might be on other grounds, an expansion of democracy abroad does not seem likely to enhance U.S. security.

The evidence and arguments this book presents also have implications for an enduring academic debate about the relative importance of domestic and systemic-level variables. The comparative explanatory power of "second"- and "third"-image variables has been debated ever since the formal study of international relations began.[2] As it stands, the democratic-peace literature supports second-image explanations, because it attributes variation in peace and war partly to cross-national variation in polity types. The reinterpretation of the democratic peace in the pages that follow, however, lies firmly within the third-image or realist tradition.

The organization of this book is as follows. I examine the analytic and then the empirical foundations of the democratic-peace literature. Next, I advance and analyze an interest-based explanation of dispute-rate patterns, as well as an alternative polity-based interpretation. Finally, I summarize my findings and discuss their implications for U.S. foreign policy after the Cold War. To begin, I preview the democratic-peace literature, as well as the evidence and arguments presented in succeeding chapters.

The Democratic-Peace Literature

Results

A large number of studies find support for the existence of a democratic peace (see, e.g., Babst 1972; Bremer 1992a, 1992b, 1993; Chan 1984, 1993; Dixon 1994; Doyle 1986; Maoz and Abdolali 1989; Maoz and Russett 1993; Morgan and Campbell 1991; Owen 1994; 1997; Russett

---

[2] Although Waltz (1959) coined these terms, the concepts they reflect originated much earlier. Waltz also analyzed, as did others, the role of human nature itself (the "first" image), although attention to this factor has virtually disappeared from the international relations literature.

1993; Small and Singer 1976).[3] In this largely empirical literature, a strong consensus prevails on two related issues.[4] First, democracies rarely, if ever, engage each other in war. Second, members of pairs of democratic states are much less likely to engage each other in serious disputes short of war than are members of other pairs of states. These findings apply across the 1816–1980 period most studies analyze.[5]

The unit of analysis in studies of the democratic peace is a dyad-year— that is, an annual record of the conflict behavior of each pair of states. Pairs of states can include two democratic states, one democratic state and one nondemocratic state, or two nondemocratic states. The focus on country pairs reflects a consensus that democracies are as likely as are other states to engage in war (e.g., Bueno de Mesquita and Lalman 1992; Chan 1984; Doyle 1986; Levy 1988; Maoz and Russett 1993; Merritt and Zinnes 1991; Morgan and Schwebach 1992; Rummel 1968; Weede 1992).[6]

Some contributions to the democratic-peace literature focus exclusively on the relative incidence of war between democratic and other pairs of states (e.g., Chan 1984; Lake 1992; Ray 1993; Spiro 1994). Based on their analysis of data spanning 150 years, Zeev Maoz and Nasrin Abdolali conclude that democracies "never" fight each other (1989, 21). This finding is representative of others in this literature. As William Dixon notes, "very strong and consistent empirical evidence [exists] that wars between democracies are at most very rare events" (1994, 14).

Other studies examine the relative rates of engagement of different polities in disputes ranging from a threat to use force to an outbreak of war (e.g., Bremer 1993; Maoz and Abdolali 1989; Maoz and Russett 1993; Morgan and Campbell 1991; Morgan and Schwebach 1992; Russett 1995). Findings based on conflicts more broadly defined are similar to those based on wars alone: democratic states are significantly less

---

[3] For an excellent and comprehensive review of the democratic-peace literature, see Chan (1997).

[4] For exceptions, see, e.g., Layne (1994); Oren (1995); Spiro (1994).

[5] Exceptions exist. For example, Maoz and Abdolali (1989) find some variation in dispute-rate patterns across time. Some studies examine only the post-1945 period (e.g., Maoz and Russett 1993).

[6] Rousseau et al. (1996) suggest that this finding may be a product of the fact that democracies are less likely to challenge the status quo than are other states. For other dissents from the prevailing consensus, see Benoit (1996) and Hewitt and Wilkenfeld (1996).

likely to engage each other in these conflicts than are members of other country pairs.

Explanations

To explain their findings, students of the democratic peace typically advance one or more of three arguments. Common to these arguments is the idea that there is something about democratic states, per se, that makes them reluctant to engage each other in serious conflicts. The particular attribute that is said to explain this reluctance varies across the literature. Some studies stress the role of political culture; others emphasize the deterrent effects of trade; and still others point to the ability of democratic regimes to constrain leaders' actions abroad.

Those who assign a large role to political culture argue that a norm of peaceful conflict resolution prevails within democracies (see, e.g., Dixon 1994; Maoz and Russett 1993). This norm precludes recourse to violence to settle any disputes that may arise within democratic states. In contrast to other regime types, then, democratic polities mandate exclusive reliance on either bargaining or third-party adjudication to resolve domestic conflicts of interests.

In the political-culture explanation, the norm that governs conflict resolution within democratic states also regulates the settlement of disputes between them. If the interests of two democracies clash, each country involved expects the other to sit down at the bargaining table rather than to resort to force. A democratic peace exists, therefore, because democratic polities "externalize their domestic political norms of tolerance and compromise in their foreign relations" (Chan 1997, 77). Thus, the use of force between them is unlikely.

The second explanation of the democratic peace emphasizes the role of trade in deterring recourse to force (e.g., Doyle 1986; Oneal et al. 1996; Oneal and Ray 1996; Oneal and Russett 1997). In Kant's theory of liberal internationalism, a "cosmopolitan law" acknowledges the "right of a foreigner not to be treated with hostility when he arrives on someone else's territory" (cited in Doyle 1986, 1158). This right applies, in particular, to those engaged in trade.

Democratic states, therefore, will maintain lower trade barriers than will nondemocracies. All other things equal, then, democracies will trade more with each other than do other states. Because the costs of trade disruption are assumed to be a linear function of the volume of trade, the opportunity costs of conflict are higher for members of pairs of democratic states than they are for members of other country pairs. This implies that the incidence of serious conflict between democratic states will be lower than it is between their nondemocratic counterparts.

In the structural-constraints explanation of the democratic peace, the relatively restricted autonomy of leaders of democratic states plays a central role: that is, a plethora of institutions exists that prevents would-be renegade leaders of democratic polities from embarking upon military adventures abroad (see, e.g., Doyle 1983; Russett 1993). Among them are opposition parties, periodic elections, and the presence of a legislature. These institutions empower political actors to sanction heads of states who choose to pursue their private interests rather than the public interest.

As in the political-culture explanation, institutionalized checks and balances influence relations not only within but also between democracies. In the event of a conflict of interests, each leader involved recognizes that the other's behavior is as constrained as his own. Thus, neither will face a temptation to launch a preemptive strike. As a result, negotiation can substitute for violence as a means of resolving conflicts.

THE MICROFOUNDATIONS OF THE DEMOCRATIC PEACE: AN ANALYSIS

Here I summarize my conclusions about the logic of these explanations, based on detailed analyses of them that appear in chapter 2. I argue that it can be very difficult and, sometimes, impossible to distinguish norm-based behavior from that which is based on interests. For reasons that are described in the next chapter, this applies a fortiori to norms of conflict resolution. Here a brief example unrelated to the democratic peace may help to make the general point clear.

Examining the relative dearth of free riding in certain societies, Douglass C. North contends that only a belief in the "legitimacy of the existing system" can explain it. He states, for example, that if everyone "believes in the 'sanctity' of a person's home, houses will remain unlocked while vacant without fear of vandalism or burglary" (North 1981, 53). But an alternative, interest-based interpretation of open-door policies seems just as compelling and much simpler.

That is, a prospective thief might reasonably be expected to calculate his expected utility from theft (i.e., the probability of not getting caught

7

multiplied by the utility of the goods he steals minus the probability of capture multiplied by the disutility of the penalty applied). Depending on the relevant probabilities and applicable rewards or punishments, he may find that he will be better off if he opts for another line of work, whether or not he believes in the sanctity of homes. Yet, based on observable behavior alone, it is impossible to discern whether norms or interests motivated his choice of action.

While this same problem need not apply universally, it does apply to behavior more generally. For example, the resolution of conflicts without recourse to force, whether within or between states, may be a product of adherence to a norm regarding appropriate methods of resolving conflict. It may also, however, be a product of the self-interests of the parties involved. In this case, as in the North example, it is impossible to deduce motivations for behavior from the behavior itself. Thus, the political-culture explanation of the democratic peace is problematic.

The same is true of the trade-based explanation. The conditions under which trade can deter conflict are much more restrictive than is usually assumed. If competitive markets exist, trade disruption will not impose significant costs on the parties to a dispute. Even in cases in which asymmetric market power exists, both the state in possession of market power and its trading partner have incentives to continue trading with each other in the event a conflict occurs between them. In addition, many empirical studies find that trade flows are no higher between democracies than between nondemocracies (e.g., Gowa 1994; Gowa and Mansfield 1993; Mansfield and Bronson 1997).

In the case of the structural-constraint explanation, the literature overstates the ability of democratic polities to affect significantly the incentives of leaders intent on maximizing their private rather than the public interest. For example, the literature does not consider the possibility that political-market failures can drive a wedge between the principles and practices of checks-and-balance systems. Yet, asymmetries in the distribution of power and the incentive structure that the production of public goods creates can lead political markets to fail. Nor does the structural-constraint explanation consider the informal substitutes for institutionalized checks and balances that exist in nondemocracies. For these and other reasons, de jure differences in formal constraint structures across regime types may be less consequential than the democratic-peace literature assumes.

In contrast to the norm-based explanation, the effect of structural constraints on recourse to force is readily susceptible to an empirical analysis.

This is so because it is much easier to find good measures of elections and independent legislatures than it is to find a measure that distinguishes reliably between norm- and interest-based behavior. Yet, unlike the trade case, empirical analyses about the posited effects of elections and legislatures on recourse to force abroad are rare. For these reasons, in chapter 3 I examine the effects of checks-and-balances on uses of force abroad, using data on the United States between 1870 and 1992.[7]

I find that only two control variables—national power status and the advent of the world wars—exert a consistent and significant impact on U.S. involvement in conflicts abroad. As such, these results do not provide strong support for the structural-constraint explanation of the democratic peace.

REANALYZING THE DATA

Dispute-Rate Patterns

Coauthored with Henry Farber, chapter 4 reexamines the empirical findings that constitute the foundations of the democratic-peace literature. The analyses in this chapter differ in only one major respect from earlier studies of the democratic peace. For theoretical, empirical, and statistical reasons detailed in the chapter itself, the sample is split in two: the period before 1914 and that after 1945 are examined separately.[8]

Disaggregating the sample yields results that stand in sharp contrast to those that emerge from the existing literature. As noted above, they show that war and other serious disputes between democratic states are relatively rare only during the Cold War. Between 1816 and 1913, members of pairs of democratic states are just as likely as are their nondemocratic counterparts to engage each other in war and in conflicts short of war.

It is worth noting here the range of the magnitude of the joint-democracy effect on war and dispute rates. The smallest effect is found in the pre–World War I period, where, as just noted, it is zero. Joint democracy exerts its strongest influence on dispute probabilities in the case of lower-level Cold War conflicts. In this case, it reduces the mean dispute rate for the sample as a whole by about 60 percent.[9]

---

[7] I explain the reasons I limit the discussion to the United States in chapter 3.

[8] More precisely, the sample is split into three periods: pre-1914, 1919–38, and 1945–80. Because the interwar period resembles what is an "interregnum" between international systems, however, the focus is on the pre–World War I and post–World War II periods.

[9] See table 4.6.

An Explanation

Cross-temporal variation in relative dyadic dispute-rate patterns is inconsistent with the democratic-peace hypothesis. It is, however, consistent with an explanation based on differences between the pre-1914 and post-1945 international systems. In the multipolar world that existed before World War I, common and conflicting interests between the major powers varied across time and issues. After World War II, however, the Cold War generated an enduring pattern of common interests among democratic states. This suggests that dispute rates should not differ across dyads before World War I; after 1945, however, the incidence of disputes between democratic states should be lower than it is between other states.

To test this argument requires a measure of interests. In the international relations literature, alliances are often used as a proxy for interests, because no direct measure of interests exists or can be constructed (e.g., Bueno de Mesquita 1981; Bueno de Mesquita and Lalman 1992; Dixon 1994; Siverson and Emmons 1991; Siverson and Starr 1991). To assess the extent to which the alliance measure is a good substitute for interests, I trace the evolution of major-power interests and alliance patterns in chapter 5. I conclude that the presence or absence of alliances is a good indicator of whether or not state interests coincide or conflict.

In chapter 6, therefore, I analyze alliance patterns for all states before World War I and after World War II. Before 1914, democracies ally with each other at lower rates than do other states. After 1945, the relationship inverts. Because the historical narrative in chapter 5 suggests that it would make sense to analyze separately the years before 1904, I also examine dispute-rate and alliance patterns for all countries between 1816 and 1904. The results show that in this period democracies are more likely to engage in disputes with each other and less likely to ally with each other than are members of other country pairs. As a result, the idiosyncratic character of the democratic peace that prevailed during the Cold War stands out even more clearly, as does the fragility of the foundations of a strategy of enlargement. These results makes it clear that the pre-1914 results are not the product of a relatively small sample, providing additional evidence against the democratic-peace hypothesis.

However, the conformity of dispute patterns to alliance patterns does not demonstrate that an interest-based explanation is the only plausible alternative to a polity-based explanation. Some contributors to the democratic-peace literature themselves suggest that variations among democratic polities may also explain variations in their behavior. Thus, chapter 6 also briefly examines this alternative.

In chapter 2, then, I begin by examining the logic of the explanations that the democratic-peace literature advances to support its findings.

Analytic Foundations of the Democratic Peace

IN THIS CHAPTER, I examine the microfoundations of the peace that is said to prevail between democratic polities. As I noted in chapter 1, three explanations have been offered: one emphasizes the role of norms; the second assigns the principal explanatory role to trade; and the third focuses upon the checks and balances that are embedded in democratic polities. I consider each in turn.

NORMS

Contributors to the democratic-peace literature assume that outcomes in international politics cannot be understood without reference to domestic political factors. In their view, these outcomes do not depend only upon the differences between states that result from factors such as the international distribution of power. Instead, they also depend upon state interests that are defined as a function of idiosyncratic factors related to domestic politics, including polity type.

This implies that explanations invoked to support the findings of a democratic peace should be distinct from those of third-image or realist theory. In particular, the logic of situations alone cannot determine state preferences. The latter must instead be a function in part of the domestic political organization of particular states. Because the norm-based explanation of the democratic peace does not satisfy this condition, no clear distinction exists between it and a more conventional interest-based explanation.

The existing literature defines norms as "rules for conduct that provide standards by which behavior is approved or disapproved" (Hechter 1987, 62). It assigns primary importance to the norm that governs methods of resolving conflicts within democratic polities. Proscribing recourse to force, the relevant norm legitimates as "proper" the use of third-party adjudication and bargaining as methods of conflict resolution (Morgan 1993, 198).[1]

---

[1] As Gaubatz notes, this argument does not consider whether adherence to this norm is a cause or a consequence of democracy (1996, 118).

This norm is adduced to explain peace not only within but also between democratic states. Thus, for example, Zeev Maoz and Bruce M. Russett believe that domestic norms influence international outcomes because states *"externalize . . . the norms of behavior that are developed within and characterize their domestic political processes and institutions"* (1993, 625, emphasis in original). In other words, if a norm mandates peaceful conflict resolution within states, it will also mandate the peaceful resolution of disputes between them. If two states are democratic, then, norms of peaceful conflict resolution will prevail between as within them. Hence, the democratic peace.

The assumption that this explanation and an interest-based explanation differ follows from the interpretation of norms that dominates the democratic-peace literature. In this interpretation, norms have "independent motivating power." As such, they are interpreted as "ex ante sources of action" rather than as "merely ex post rationalizations of self interest" (Elster 1989, 125).

The sharp distinction between norm- and interest-based explanations would fade, however, were proponents of the democratic peace to adopt another interpretation of norms. For example, some contributors to the more general literature on norms believe that the latter reflect self-interest. In their view, it is the expectation of external sanctions that motivates both the internalization of norms and adherence to them (Scott 1971, xiii). As a result, as Elster observes, norms "may appear to cause cooperative behavior when in fact the relationship is spurious, with both norms and behavior being influenced by common interests" (1989, 233).

In this view, it is interests that drive norms, and little, if anything, distinguishes between them. If this were the conception of norms that prevailed in the democratic-peace literature, the role assigned to peaceful dispute resolution could be recast in terms of the interests of states and the logic of their situations. More specifically, a revealed preference for nonviolent methods of resolving conflicts, whether at home or abroad, could be seen as reflecting its relative price rather than its normative appeal: bargaining is less costly than war, whether civil or international (Fearon 1992; Powell 1990).[2]

This, in turn, would raise the issue of whether it makes sense to assume that a preference for peaceful methods of conflict resolution is unique to

---

[2] Indeed, this recasting makes it easy to understand the interest of states in settling disputes short of war, while rendering problematic their failure to do so. Fearon advances the imperfect process of signaling resolve as a candidate explanation of war (1992; 1994).

democratic polities. After all, very few in any polity, including heads of states, can be expected to prosper absent a presumption that nonviolent means will be relied upon to settle domestic disputes. As Mancur Olson observes, incentives to produce any "good that could be taken by others" will be very weak if recourse to force is common. As a result, the provision of domestic order creates "colossal" gains not only for social welfare but also for the well-being of leaders, irrespective of the polities they govern (Olson 1993, 567).[3]

Thus, the norm-based explanation of the democratic peace does not necessarily differ from its more conventional interest-based counterpart. The argument that a preference for peaceful methods of conflict resolution is unique to leaders of democratic polities is not robust to the adoption of a standard, albeit different, interpretation of norms than that which dominates the democratic-peace literature. As a result, it cannot explain the democratic peace: if many polities have a preference for resolving domestic conflicts peacefully, the externalization of these preferences will not distinguish the behavior of members of democratic dyads from that of members of other country pairs.

I turn next to an analysis of trade as an explanation of the peace that is said to prevail between democratic polities.

Trade

Trade-based explanations of the relationship between polities and peace echo the large literature on interdependence that emerged in the early 1970s and 1980s (see, e.g., Vernon 1971). Some contributors to that literature emphasized the pacific effects of trade. As the exchange of goods and services between states increased, they noted, the opportunity costs of disputes between them also increased (Gasiorowski 1986; Gasiorowski and Polachek 1982; Polachek 1980). Thus, increasing economic interdependence should decrease the incidence of international conflict.[4]

In the variant of this argument that the democratic-peace literature adopts (see, e.g., Doyle 1986; Oneal and Russett 1997), interdependence exerts an especially strong effect on the probability of peace be-

---

[3] Indeed, because of their "encompassing interest" in maximizing economic output, Olson suggests, leaders of authoritarian polities may have even stronger incentives to provide a peaceful order than do their democratic counterparts (1993, 569).

[4] For an excellent critique of the interdependence literature, see Baldwin (1980). Also see Cooper (1968; 1972).

tween democratic polities. This is so because, in Kant's words, the "cosmopolitan right to hospitality" that democracies accord to each other allows "the 'spirit of commerce' sooner or later to take hold of every nation" (cited in Doyle 1986, 1161). Thus, democracies are less likely to erect barriers to trade than are other states. As a result, trade flows between democratic states will be higher than are those between other states, making conflict more costly for the former than for the latter states. All else equal, then, the incidence of conflict should be lower between democracies than between members of other country pairs.

There are two problems with this argument. First, it seems clear that the "spirit of commerce" has not dominated the competing interests of all members of democratic polities across time. Import-competing industries that file petitions for protection do not discriminate between the exports of democracies and those of nondemocracies.[5] Nor is there any evidence that elected officials discriminate in this way when they supply tariffs or nontariff barriers to trade (NTBs) in response to these petitions or to other demands for protection (see, e.g., Goldstein 1993; Gourevitch 1986; Magee, Brock and Young 1989; Rogowski 1989; Schattschneider 1935). The "spirit of commerce" may exist, but its appeal is not irresistible.

Thus, it is not surprising that empirical analyses of available trade data do not find strong and consistent evidence that trade flows are higher between democracies than between other states. Edward D. Mansfield and I examined the impact of political factors on bilateral trade flows between major powers in a series of cross sections between 1905 and 1985. We found that whether or not the trading partners were both democracies mattered in only one case (Gowa 1994; Gowa and Mansfield 1993, 416). Extending the analysis to a larger sample of countries during the post–World War II period, Mansfield and Rachel Bronson (1997) found no consistent relationship between regime type and trade flows across time.[6]

Second, even if the results of an analysis of a larger sample of states across a longer time span showed that members of democratic pairs of

---

[5] All else equal, if trade were, in fact, higher between democracies than between members of other country pairs, import-competing industries would target the exports of democratic states more frequently than they would the goods that nondemocracies export.

[6] More precisely, they found that, although trade flows between democracies are higher than are those between other states between 1950 and 1965, no difference exists thereafter. Mansfield and Bronson attribute the positive relationship they observe in the early postwar years to the influence of the Cold War.

states traded consistently more with each other than did members of other country pairs, the conclusion that trade reduces the probability of conflict between them would not necessarily follow. If competitive markets exist, any disruption of trade between two states will simply lead both to alternative markets. The costs incurred in the process will be limited to the transaction costs that accompany market shifting. However, if both states incur roughly comparable costs, each would have an incentive to continue to trade with the other as long as it is feasible to do so.

Suppose, for example, that a serious diplomatic dispute breaks out between France and Germany. Suppose, in addition, that France imports all of its widgets from Germany and that Germany imports all of its goat cheese from France. Suppose also that the French demand for widgets and the German demand for goat cheese are highly inelastic, perhaps because the French cannot produce wine without widgets and the productivity of German labor depends upon goat-cheese consumption. Will this exchange of widgets and cheese exercise a strong influence on the probability that a Franco-German dispute will escalate to one that involves either the threat to use force or its actual use?

It will do so if and only if France has no other source of widgets or Germany no other source of goat cheese or if one country cannot find alternative markets for its exports. That is, the threat of a breakdown of bilateral trade can act as a powerful deterrent only if France or Germany possesses monopoly or monopsony power in widget or cheese markets. Otherwise, France can import its widgets and Germany its cheese from other countries, and each country can find export markets in third countries. Alternatively, unless conflict renders the logistics of trade impossible, France and Germany might choose to continue to exchange widgets and cheese to avoid the deadweight loss each would incur in shifting markets.[7]

Thus, as the literature on economic sanctions more generally makes clear (see, e.g., Baldwin 1985; Kaempfer and Lowenberg 1992; Martin 1992), a disruption of trade between two countries, whether incident upon an armed dispute between them or for other reasons, can inflict large welfare costs only in cases in which alternative markets do not exist. When competitive markets exist, therefore, trade should not be expected to influence the probability of international disputes.[8]

---

[7] In a preliminary analysis, Barbieri and Levy (1998) find that war can sometimes leave trade flows unaffected or even increase them.

[8] Oneal and Russett (1997) report that increasing trade does diminish the incidence of

Indeed, neither party to an armed dispute may have an incentive to disrupt trade even in the absence of competitive markets. If both states have equivalent degrees of market power, a decision to disrupt trade in the event of conflict would be self-defeating: it will leave both countries worse off (Johnson 1953–54). Thus, even if France and Germany were engaged in an armed dispute with each other, they might continue to exchange cheese and widgets. If either chose to do otherwise, it would simply be shooting itself in the foot: it would inflict as much injury on itself as on its opponent.[9]

Nor does the existence of asymmetric market power affect this decision calculus. Presumably, a state able to improve its terms of trade unilaterally would have done so ex ante. If it had waited to do so until the outbreak of conflict, in the interim it would have inflicted costs upon itself in the form of foregone increases in its real income. Similarly, if its trading partner had had a more profitable alternative ex ante, it would have adopted it. As in the symmetric case, then, disrupting trade in goods and services when the distribution of market power is asymmetric will impose costs on both sides.

The logic of this argument applies as well to cases in which monopoly or monopsony power originates in a relation-specific investment. The latter, as Beth V. and Robert M. Yarbrough note, is an investment "undertaken to be used in specific transactions with a specific partner." Because its value in other transactions is either negligible or nonexistent, a relation-specific investment can endow a would-be belligerent with the requisite market power to improve its terms of trade (Yarbrough and Yarbrough 1992, 25).

For example, Japanese investors might design a plant to build cars specifically to meet the demands of the U.S. market. In doing so, they become vulnerable to a U.S. holdup. Once the plant is built, the U.S. government can seek to renegotiate the terms of the agreement, because it is impossible for the owners of the plant to relocate it profitably. Other examples of relation-specific investments include cross-national upstream or downstream integration of a firm.[10]

As in the case of market power more generally, relation-specific investments may not have any effect upon the probability that a dispute will

---

interstate conflict. Beck, Katz, and Tucker (1997), however, find that this result is not robust to a correction for the existence of temporal dependence.

[9] This assumes that the utility each country assigns to trade is based only upon its effects on its economic welfare.

[10] For a good discussion of these and other examples, see Yarbrough and Yarbrough (1992).

escalate. Investors should be aware ex ante of the danger of reneging. As such, they will attempt to minimize the ex post danger of a holdup via contingent contracts or the establishment of a bilateral monopoly. If neither is possible, attempts to renege will be difficult to deter.

However, it is not clear that the onset of a serious conflict will have any effect on these attempts. Absent an effective deterrent mechanism, either party to a relation-specific investment will execute a holdup as soon as it becomes feasible, for the same reason that states with asymmetric market power seek to exploit their power as quickly as possible.

If reputational concerns had deterred holdups prior to the initiation of a conflict, however, the actual outbreak of armed conflict may precipitate opportunistic acts that would not have otherwise occurred. This is so because a reputation for reneging during armed conflicts is unlikely to be very costly, given the infrequency with which such conflicts occur. In this case, the escalation of a dispute may, in fact, inflict trade-related costs on its potential belligerents.

Whether it will do so depends, however, upon the distribution of relation-specific investments. Although no direct evidence is available about this distribution, the logic of rational expectations suggests that these investments will be made in countries that are unlikely to engage in serious disputes with the home country, all else being equal. This suggests that, as in the case of trade, investments will be skewed toward countries allied with the home country.[11]

Because armed disputes between allied countries are relatively rare, opportunism related to such disputes is also likely to be rare.[12] Also, as in the cases discussed above, if each party to a dispute has made comparable relation-specific investments in the other and each can exert some control over the renegotiation of contracts, no holdups should occur in the event either of a war or of a serious dispute short of war: opportunism would only make both belligerents worse off.

Thus, explanations of the relationship between peace and polities that place trade at their core do not seem compelling. There is no systematic empirical evidence that democracies engage in more trade with each other than do members of other country pairs. Moreover, even if they did, it is not at all obvious that higher levels of trade would lead to lower levels of conflicts: the conditions under which they might do so are much

---

[11] For evidence about the trade case, see Gowa (1994); Gowa and Mansfield (1993).

[12] More precisely, controlling for contiguity, allies are less likely to engage in conflicts with each other than are nonallied states (Bremer 1992b).

more restrictive than trade-based explanations of the democratic peace assume.[13]

CHECKS AND BALANCES

The premise of the checks-and-balances explanation is that much more effective domestic political constraints on leaders exist in democratic than in other polities (e.g., Lake 1992; cf. Morgan and Campbell 1991). The result is to deter the use of force abroad, because of its distributional effects: the benefits of using military power accrue to leaders, while its costs are dispersed among the population.

As such, the argument is the clear intellectual descendant of that advanced by Immanuel Kant long ago. In states that are not republics,[14] Kant maintains, a decision to wage war is the "easiest thing in the world to decide upon, because war does not require of the ruler, who is the proprietor and not a member of the state, the least sacrifice of the pleasure of his table, the chase, his country houses, his court functions, and the like" (cited in Doyle 1983, 229).[15]

As in the case of the norm-based explanation and for much the same reason, systems of checks and balances within democratic states are also said to explain the dynamics of disputes between them. When the interests of democratic states conflict, as Bueno de Mesquita and Lalman note, "each has unusually high confidence that the other is likely to be constrained to be averse to the use of force." This "encourages states under all but the most unusual circumstances to negotiate with one another or to accept the status quo" (1992, 156–7).

This explanation is less compelling than it might appear at first glance, for three complementary reasons. First, informal substitutes for institutionalized checks and balances exist in other polities. Second, nonmyopic leaders can relax constraints on their behavior. Third, political-market

---

[13] This logic may explain why civil wars have occurred more frequently than international wars since 1945, despite the presumably very high levels of trade that occur within national boundaries (Gaddis 1986, 112).

[14] Kant refers specifically to republics (i.e., systems in which the rule of law governs and all individuals' basic rights are recognized). For a brief discussion of the distinction between republics and democracies, see Chan (1997, 61).

[15] Not all contributors to the democratic-peace literature agree, however. As Ray points out, war "does not often directly affect the 'table,' 'hunt,' or 'places of pleasure' . . . of, say, American presidents or British prime ministers any more than it affects those of autocratic leaders" (1995, 3).

failures create a wedge between the "blueprints" that democracies are built upon and the political processes that operate within them (Przeworski 1991, 103).[16] I discuss each of these in turn.

Informal Substitutes

The democratic-peace literature seems to assume that the autonomy of leaders of nondemocracies is unbounded. Yet, the tenure in office of these leaders depends upon some "selectorate"—that is, on some supporting coalition of interests. As long as the preferences of its members differ, a nonelected leader who uses force abroad to pursue his private interests can sacrifice his incumbency, not to mention his life, in the process (Morgan and Campbell 1991, 190). Thus, in the absence of data about the preference distributions of selectorates in democratic and nondemocratic polities, it is impossible to establish whether the need for domestic support imposes tighter constraints on leaders of one regime type than on another.[17]

Some leaders of nondemocracies also confront a constraint on their ability to wage war that is unique to them,[18] that is, the construction of strong military forces can place their incumbencies at risk. If the armed forces are strong enough to defeat foreign adversaries, they may also be strong enough to overthrow their nominal commander-in-chief. Maintaining only weak armed forces, however, creates a risk of a takeover by rivals to rule outside the state. Heads of states of nondemocratic polities, therefore, confront a dilemma that does not plague leaders of democracies. This dilemma may make rulers of these states more interested in reducing the incidence of wars than in waging them.

The founding principles of the Organization of African Unity (OAU) illustrate the importance nondemocratic leaders can place on this problem. Its prospective member states did not have large indigenous military units in place. If each of them agreed to respect the borders of all others, as Gordon Tullock notes, all would be able "to keep relatively small mili-

[16] As Chan points out, explanations of the democratic peace that emphasize structural constraints on the autonomy of leaders also neglect the "institutional incentives that incline them to be more belligerent than they otherwise would be" (1997, 78). See also Owen (1994).

[17] See, e.g., Morgan and Campbell, who argue that variation in the efficacy of different types of constraints suggests that the autonomy of leaders of nondemocracies may be lower than that of their democratic counterparts (1991, 192–93).

[18] This discussion is based on Tullock (1987).

tary units, and what is more important, military units that are weak" (1987, 37). As a result, the founding states agreed that a pledge to adhere to preexisting borders would be a prerequisite of membership in the OAU. To the extent that the organization conferred excludable benefits, then, the OAU could facilitate collusion among incumbent African leaders to preserve their incumbency.

Myopic and Nonmyopic Leaders

The structural-constraint explanation casts would-be renegade leaders as myopic, passive actors. In doing so, it exaggerates the ability of formal constraints to abridge the freedom of action of leaders. This is so because farsighted leaders will attempt to anticipate and preempt opposition to their decisions to use force abroad.

The design of institutions of conscription provides a good example of the instruments available to leaders seeking to minimize domestic constraints on their exercise of military power. A universal conscription system is often a very attractive option, if all-volunteer forces are infeasible.[19] The appeal of such a system inheres in its almost inevitable evolution into a selective-service system. Universal induction would impede the production of goods and services necessary to prosecute the war as well as draft those physically or mentally unfit for military service.[20]

Thus, a nominally universal system generates with certainty both deferments and exemptions. As such, it allows political leaders to skew the allocation of free rides toward potential conscripts who ex ante seem most capable of effective political opposition. Although a dearth of data precludes a systematic empirical analysis of the distribution of deferments and exemptions,[21] anecdotal evidence from a variety of countries across time indicates that political leaders have long sought to supply avenues of escape to those most likely to oppose service in the armed forces.[22]

---

[19] For an excellent analysis of the politics of conscription across nations and time, see Levi (1997).

[20] Exemptions on the basis of fitness have, of course, their own, possibly unintended consequences. During World War I, for example, these standards led so many prospective draftees to have "their teeth extracted that the War Department publicly warned that dentists could be prosecuted for aiding draft evasion" (Baskir and Strauss 1978, 19).

[21] See Levi (1997) for further discussion of data problems in this area.

[22] Deferments and exemptions do not exhaust the options available to would-be free riders. Draft evasion is another obvious alternative, as is desertion. Less obviously, some conscripts can simply decline to engage the enemy in combat. During World War I, for

21

Because of the correlation between political participation and income (Lijphart 1997, 1), the distribution of free rides tends to favor higher-income, better-educated members of the draft-age population.[23] France, for example, pioneered the replacement system in 1793, allowing a potential conscript to supply a substitute to serve in his stead. Adopted by Sweden, Holland, Spain, Belgium, and other European countries, the French system supplied both the necessary troop complements and "an alternative to propertied citizens who might otherwise resist conscription politically, avoid the draft altogether, or desert" (Levi 1997, 88).[24] Similarly, during the U.S. Civil War, a prospective Union conscript could avoid the draft if he either paid $300[25] or found a substitute to serve in his place.[26] During the Vietnam War, President Johnson decreased the measured intelligence level required to enter the armed services, partly to avoid drafting college students (Baskir and Strauss 1977, 17; Curry 1985, 53–5; Moskos 1969, 157).[27]

---

example, troops deployed in the trenches often ignored official entreaties to engage the enemy, preferring to reduce their risk of death by establishing tacit truces across front lines (Ashworth 1980). Similarly, S. L. A. Marshall found that most of the World War II infantry troops he interviewed ignored the enemy "even when his person presented a clear target" cited in Ashworth (1980, 214). And, during the Korean War, Roger Little reports, a "highly solidary 'buddy' system" emerged, which stigmatized those who conformed to and rewarded those who deviated from the behavior that the official chain of command designated as "heroic" (cited in Ashworth 1980, 219).

[23] This distribution can also be explained on efficiency grounds. It may be more costly to the nation to induct individuals with relatively large endowments of human capital than to draft those with less. It is not at all obvious, however, why the objective functions of political officials in the case at hand should differ from those more typically assigned to them: that is, maximizing their self-interest.

[24] Substitution and replacement systems, as Levi notes, were "win-win, permitting those who preferred to avoid military service to pay a supplement to someone else who perceived this as a reasonable alternative" (1997, 93).

[25] In 1863, $300 was 75 percent of a "workingman's" annual salary (Geary 1991, 103).

[26] Manpower shortages prompted Congress to consider allowing conscription in defeated areas in the South. Because of the distributional implications involved, this provoked a heated debate. Some representatives insisted that credit for the individuals so impressed be divided among all states equally. Otherwise, they feared, the relatively wealthy New England states would benefit disproportionately from this extension of conscription. For an excellent discussion of attempts by congressional representatives to shift the burden of the Civil War draft onto states other than those they represented, see Geary (1991).

[27] As of mid-1968, about 40 percent of those admitted under "Project 100,000" auspices were nonwhites; more than half had not completed high school (Moskos 1969, 172). Baskir and Strauss estimate that Vietnam student deferments led to an overall increase of about 6.5 percent in male college enrollments (1978, 29).

In addition, the allocation of those inducted into the service also privileges those with higher endowments. Ground combat forces in the Korean War, for example, were "mainly" composed of relative low socio-economic groups (Moskos 1970, 16). Similarly, during the Vietnam War, the relatively poor and less educated were more likely to end up in the ground combat forces than in other branches (Segal 1989, 35).

As these examples suggest, leaders of democratic and other polities do not respond passively to anticipated attempts to impede their actions abroad. Instead they adopt wide-ranging strategies to relax what they foresee as possible constraints on their freedom of action. Just before the Canadian general elections of 1917, for example, the government passed legislation that gave it "considerable leeway in assigning the votes of service personnel to any riding it chose"; enfranchised "close female relatives of military personnel and servicewomen (giving some women the vote for the first time in a federal election)"; and disenfranchised both conscientious objectors and naturalized citizens born in enemy countries (Levi 1997, 120). As a result of these and other actions taken by non-myopic leaders, systems of checks and balances do not seem to operate as effectively as the democratic-peace literature assumes.

Political-Market Failures

Finally, the structural-constraint explanation neglects the wedge that asymmetries in the distribution of political power, public goods, and principal-agent problems drive between the de jure and de facto operation of democratic polities (e.g., Cox 1990; Cukierman and Meltzer 1986; Fiorina and Noll 1978; Persson and Tabellini 1990; Rogoff 1990; Rogoff and Sibert 1988; Weingast, Shepsle, and Johnson 1981).

At the most basic level, a uniform distribution of the right to exercise one's voice does not ensure a uniform distribution of the effective expression of voice. As noted above, political participation is a luxury good: both income and education correlate with voting and even more strongly with other types of political engagement (Lijphart 1997, 1). This is so partly because resource expenditures are necessary to overcome the collective-action problems that can impede the effective operation of voice.

One effect of this gap between the de jure distribution and the de facto exercise of political rights in democratic polities, as Adam Smith observed long ago, is to produce foreign policies that are inimical to the nation as a whole. In the case of imperialism, for example, Smith noted that "to found a great empire for the sole purpose of raising up a people of customers may at first sight appear a project fit only for a nation of shop-keepers." In reality, however, he added, "it is a project altogether unfit for a nation of shopkeepers; but extremely fit for a nation whose government is influenced by shopkeepers" (cited in Ekelund and Tollison 1981, 10).

That this same dynamic characterizes other foreign-policy processes at different points in time is clear. The logic of Smith's argument is amply evident in foreign economic policy, for example. Trade barriers exist in many democracies, despite their adverse effects on aggregate economic welfare. They do so because import protection produces concentrated benefits and diffuse costs: import-competing producers gain; consumers lose. Because producers can organize more easily than can consumers,[28] special-interest groups seeking import barriers are staple elements of the trade policy process.[29]

As a result, so are legislators, particularly in single-member district systems. Aware that voters regard them as "ombudsmen and brokers" and evaluate them ex ante, as well as ex post, as service providers, legislators actively engage issues related to trade policy in response to the interests of their import-competing constituents (Fiorina 1981, 210).[30]

Collective-action problems also exist in the realm of decisions about using military force abroad, although they disenfranchise groups as well as individuals. As in the trade-barrier case, the net benefits of using military power are not uniformly distributed. The costs of using force tend to be concentrated on a relatively small group. More than 95 percent of disputes involving the United States in the last century, for example, re-

---

[28] McChesney (1997) advances a different argument about the lack of organized consumer representation. Rational consumers, he argues, do not oppose producers' extraction of rents. If they did so successfully, McChesney contends, they would forever be vulnerable to political threats to their surplus, making their potential losses higher than if they allow producers to prevail.

[29] They are also staple elements of a series of papers about endogenous-tariff theory and practice. See, e.g., Bohara and Kaempfer (1991); Grossman and Helpman (1995); Hansen (1990); Lohmann and O'Halloran (1994); and McKeown (1984).

[30] That their responses take the form of trade barriers rather than income subsidies, however, has long puzzled students of trade politics. Dixit and Londregan (1995) suggest that these suboptimal transfers occur because voters and legislators cannot make credible commitments to each other with respect to the exchange of income and votes across time. Dixit (1996, 110–11) adds that if, as Katzenstein (1985) argues, small countries can use more efficient adjustment mechanisms, it may be because their size and relative homogeneity allows them to undertake the monitoring that can make intertemporal commitments credible.

sulted in fewer than one thousand casualties for all belligerent states.[31] In contrast to the trade case, however, the members of this group are ex ante unknown. Thus, a classic public-good problem arises: those who will bear the costs of and those who stand to gain from political action to oppose the use of force may be members of nonoverlapping sets.[32] Thus, prohibitively high barriers to collective action can confront those opposed to the use of military power abroad.

As a result, legislators also have relatively weak incentives to engage heads of state on these issues. Their incentives are further diluted because of a public-good problem among legislators themselves: while the costs to a legislator of opposing the use of force accrue to him alone, the benefits of his action are widely dispersed. When electoral success depends to a large extent on the delivery of district-specific benefits, legislators are unlikely to expend scarce resources on the production of this, as on other, public goods (Cox 1990; Mayhew 1974).

A Caveat

Strategic leaders and a skewed distribution of political resource endowments do not, of course, exhaust the constraints on military adventures abroad that institutionalized checks-and-balance systems can impose. Among the most notable omissions is the existence of periodic elections, perhaps the most potent means to ensure the accountability of leaders to their publics.

If voters are more reluctant to deploy military power than are leaders, as the democratic-peace literature assumes, and they have complete information about foreign policy, the prospect of elections should constrain a leader's recourse to force.

Public-opinion surveys, however, consistently show that voters are not well informed about foreign policy. In addition, the premise that private information exists is much more common than is the assumption that complete information prevails. Fearon (1992; 1994), for example, suggests that democratic states can more easily demonstrate their resolve during a dispute, because voters and leaders have asymmetric information

---

[31] This statistic is derived from the Correlates of War Militarized Interstate Dispute (MID) data set, discussed in detail in chapter 3.

[32] A large theoretical and empirical literature exists on the Prisoners' Dilemma (PD) games that contributions to a public good involve. For good introductions to the political science literature on PD games, see, e.g., Axelrod (1984); Hardin (1982); Oye (1985).

about crisis bargaining.[33] Private information is also essential to Gelpi's finding that the diversionary use of force abroad is "generally a pathology of democratic states" (1997b, 277). Alastair Smith concurs: in his analysis of the use of force, he assumes that the existence of asymmetric information biases leaders toward using military power abroad as elections approach (1996). Downs and Rocke (1994; 1995) argue that the combination of imminent elections and incomplete information can encourage leaders to continue to wage war. Thus, it seems that elections can as easily encourage as restrain would-be renegade leaders.

Indeed, that elections and the use of force are directly related is implied by the "rally-round-the flag" literature (e.g., Callahan and Virtanen 1993; Gaubatz 1991; Hess and Orphanides 1995; James and Oneal 1991; Levy 1988; MacKuen 1983; Marra, Ostrom, and Simon 1990; Morgan and Bickers 1992; Mueller 1970; 1973; 1994; Oneal, Lian, and Joyner 1996; Ostrom, Simon, and Job 1986; Stoll 1984). Because a rally event—that is, a "specific, dramatic, and sharply focused" international event (Mueller 1973, 209)—creates a short-run surge of public opinion in favor of the incumbent,[34] it seems to create opportunities for incumbents to use force abroad as an instrument of political campaigns at home (Ostrom and Simon 1985).

Conclusion

In sum, existing explanations of the democratic peace seem to rest on weak microfoundations. The role of norms and interests in motivating behavior can be very difficult to distinguish. Only a tenuous logic supports the claim that trade is a strong deterrent to conflict. Political-market failures seem to create a wedge between the de jure and de facto operation of checks and balances: skewed political participation, public-good problems, and asymmetric information all appear to compromise the efficacy of democratic institutions.

An empirical analysis of norms creates a "daunting methodological

---

[33] Democracies are endowed with this advantage, Fearon suggests, because domestic political audiences will punish leaders who back down. This assumes, however, that constituents do not understand the logic of crisis bargaining, but that leaders (and academics) do. Yet, as all poker players and parents know, backing down can sometimes be the optimal course of action. This same statement would seem to apply to most, if not all, voters. Why, then, would constituents punish leaders whose bluffs are sometimes called?

[34] For exceptions, see, e.g., Edwards (1990); Edwards and Swenson (1997).

challenge," as Elster observes, because "it is crucial to control for self-interest when trying to ascertain the impact of norms" (1989, 233). Empirical analyses of the effect of democratic polities on trade are relatively common. Few, if any, empirical analyses exist about the posited effects of both elections and legislatures, however. In the next chapter, therefore, I present an empirical analysis of the impact of checks and balances at home on the use of force abroad.

Legislators, Voters, and the Use of Force Abroad

IN THIS CHAPTER, I examine whether independent legislatures and elections influence the use of force abroad. I do so because the extent to which the practices conform to the principles of democratic polities is unclear. In addition, systematic empirical analyses of the structural-constraint explanation are rare, and those that do exist have generated weak and inconsistent results. Morgan and Campbell (1991), for example, find that executive-legislative parity does not have a consistently significant effect on dispute escalation. Leeds and Davis (1997) report that elections and the propensity of democratic states to engage in international disputes are unrelated.[1] Gaubatz (1991), however, finds that the advent of elections depresses the war rates of democratic states, while Hess and Orphanides (1995) report that U.S. initiation and escalation rates double when elections are pending during recessions.

For several reasons, I limit this analysis to the United States. The United States is the only democratic state that has assumed each of the three possible values of national-power status, an important control variable. It is also one among very few democratic states in which elections are held at fixed intervals, eliminating the endogeneity problem that otherwise exists between the use of force and the timing of elections (Gaubatz 1997, 152). In addition, U.S. legislators and presidents are elected independently of each other, allowing national elections to operate as referenda on the president's performance. Finally, the U.S. constitution lodges the power to declare war in Congress, precisely because of the distributional effects that the democratic-peace literature emphasizes.[2]

---

[1] As Gaubatz (1991) and Smith (1996) suggest, Leeds and Davis find that the relationship between the use of force and domestic polities can be attributed to the decisions of other countries to refrain from acting against democratic states when the latter might be predisposed to respond aggressively (1997, 831).

[2] As James Madison observed in the "Helvidius" essays, for example, the lodging of the power to declare war in Congress rather than in the executive should decrease the incidence of war, because "war is the true nurse of executive aggrandizement. In war, a physical force is to be created; and it is the executive will which is to direct it. In war the public treasures are to be unlocked; and it is the executive hand which is to dispense them. . . . It is in war,

Limiting the analysis to the United States, of course, has a cost: the results may not apply across all democratic states. However, that the analysis here uses data from only one country does not diminish its relevance to the democratic-peace literature. The latter assumes that common knowledge of the existence of structural constraints determines the dispute dynamics of members of democratic dyads. For this effect to occur, however, it must be the case that these systems actually operate as intended. The purpose of this chapter is to examine whether, in fact, they do so.

It is also important to note that the absence of cross-polity variation in war rates does not affect the significance of this analysis. That average war rates are the same across regime types does not mean that no cross-polity differences exist with respect to the determinants of these rates. For example, war may covary in democratic polities with electoral cycles or with the extent of legislative independence. A correlation between these covariates across democracies would establish another possible source of a democratic peace.

RESEARCH DESIGN

The Sample

With very few exceptions (Gaubatz 1991; Hess and Orphanides 1995), studies of the effects of politics at home on the use of force abroad examine only the post–World War II period. This period, however, is unique in several respects. For example, the United States emerged as one of two superpowers after World War II. As such, postwar presidents may have had more freedom to use force abroad than their predecessors enjoyed.[3]

Here I examine U.S. recourse to force between 1870 and 1992. There are two reasons to begin in 1870. First, the U.S. political system stabilizes at about this time. After the Civil War, shifts in domestic politics led to changes within, rather than the replacement of, the basic U.S. political structure (Poole and Rosenthal 1991, 229). Second, recent estimates of U.S. gross national product, which I use to construct a control variable, are available only as of 1869 (Balke and Gordon 1989; Romer 1989).

---

finally, that laurels are to be gathered; and it is the executive brow they are to encircle (cited in Fisher 1995, 21).

[3] For a discussion of other unusual attributes of the post–World War II period directly related to the issue of domestic incentives to use military force, see Marra, Ostrom, and Simon (1990, 592, 620).

To define and measure U.S. engagements in armed disputes annually, I rely upon the Small and Singer Correlates of War (COW) data set on Militarized Interstate Disputes (MIDs).[4] This data set interprets broadly the set of events that might be described as uses of force. Thus, an international event classifies as a MID if it involves overt "government-sanctioned" "threats to use military force, displays of military force, . . . actual uses of force," or war (Gochman and Maoz 1984, 587).

Defined as "verbal indications of hostile intent," threats are "contingent and usually take the form of an ultimatum" that military force will follow unless compliance is forthcoming. Displays "involve military demonstrations but no combat interactions," for example, shows of troops, border fortifications, and nuclear alerts. Defined as "active military involvement," uses of force include blockades, territorial occupations, seizures of "material or personnel of official forces," clashes, and raids. Common to all three is the risk of war, defined as a clash that results in a minimum of one thousand battle fatalities (Jones, Bremer, and Singer 1996, 168–73).

The original MID data set includes disputes that occurred between 1870 and 1976. It records the United States as involved in 123 MIDs during this period. A recently revised version of this data set extends coverage through 1992. According to these data, the United States is involved in 196 MIDs from 1870 through 1976, as well as in 68 disputes in the succeeding 16 years. The changes seem to reflect a more extensive use of secondary sources rather than a change in coding rules. As a result, I use the revised MID data here. Table 3.1 summarizes the data.[5]

The broad range of disputes in the COW data permits a test of whether the results of the reported empirical analyses are robust to differ-

---

[4] Part 3 of ICPSR Study Number 9044. Other studies use the International Crisis Behavior (ICB) data set (e.g., Brecher and Wilkenfeld 1982; Brecher, Wilkenfeld, and James 1989; Lian and Oneal 1993; Marra, Ostrom, and Simon 1990; Ostrom, Simon, and Job 1986; Stoll 1984) or some subset of the data in a 1978 Brookings study (Blechman, Kaplan, and Hall 1978).

For my purposes, however, these sources are not useful: neither begins before 1918 nor draws on the most appropriate universe of cases. The Brookings study records U.S. force deployments or withdrawals abroad for political purposes between 1946 and 1975. Clausewitz notwithstanding, it excludes cases in which U.S. forces actually engaged those of another nation, interpreting these as "martial" rather than "political" uses of force. The ICB project includes only foreign-policy crises, which need not include either threats to use force or its actual use (Brecher 1993, 3; Brecher and Wilkenfeld 1982, 411).

[5] I also repeated the analyses in table 3.2 using the original MID data. The only difference that emerges is that the world war variable is less consistently significant than it is in the results reported below. Complete results are available from the author.

TABLE 3.1
Number of U.S. MIDs, 1870–1992: Hostility Levels

	Number	Percent
Threat to use force	23	8.71
Display of force	105	39.77
Use of force	71	26.89
War	7	2.65
Hostility level missing	58	21.97
Total	264	99.99

Note: These data are derived from the revised MID data set of the Correlates of War project.

ent types of MIDs. Ex ante, it is not obvious whether it makes more sense to use all MIDs or only some subset of them. On the one hand, limiting the sample to those disputes that are likely to be particularly potent instruments of partisan political competition (i.e., uses of force or wars) might make sense. On the other hand, given the risks associated with the use of force or war, lower-level conflicts might be a reelection-minded president's preferred instruments of choice (e.g., Russett 1990, 45–46). Threats to use and displays of force are, in addition, among the actions that states use to signal their resolve during crises (e.g., Fearon 1992; 1994; Powell 1996b; Schultz 1997). Because they are likely to be understood as such, they also are prospective weapons in political battles at home.

As a result, I first analyze all MIDs. Then I examine a subset that includes only MIDs that involve the use of either force or war.[6] I label this subset "MaxMIDs." I include in the all-MIDs analysis the 58 disputes that lack information about hostility levels reached. I omit these disputes from the MaxMIDs analysis, for two reasons: (1) none of them are in the COW data set on war and (2) uses of force seem less likely to be coded as missing than either threats or displays of force.

The newly revised COW data set also provides another way to differentiate between MIDs. In the original COW data, Small and Singer labeled

[6] I also analyzed separately only threats to use force and displays of force. The world war variable is insignificant in all specifications. Otherwise, the results do not vary from those reported in the text for all MIDs and are available from the author.

certain states as initiators. They warned, however, that their labels were "crude" and "tentative, resting solely on historians' consensus as to whose battalions made the first attack in strength." Indeed, they cautioned explicitly against identifying an "initiator" with the "participant [which] 'caused' the war, whether by action, threat, or other provocation" (1982, 194).

In the updated version of the MID data, Jones, Bremer, and Singer (1996) include a variable that seems intended to improve upon the quality of the initiator variable. The new variable indicates whether or not a state engaged in a dispute is "revisionist," that is, a state that is dissatisfied with the status quo and that issues an overt challenge to it.[7]

A great deal of potential added value inheres in information about whether a state is revisionist. All other things equal, a state can choose whether or not to challenge the status quo; that is, it can decide whether to assume the risk of engaging in a dispute. The decision of a state that is the target of such a challenge is more heavily constrained.

This implies that the effects of elections and legislatures on recourse to force may vary as a function of whether a state is the initiator or target of a challenge to the status quo. Neither voters nor legislators are likely to object to instances in which the president uses force in response to a challenge from abroad. They are more likely to do so in cases in which the president uses military power to challenge the status quo. Thus, the predicted effects of checks and balances should emerge more clearly in cases in which U.S. behavior conforms to that of a revisionist state. As a result, these cases seem particularly appropriate to this analysis.

Jones, Bremer, and Singer report that they made a "great effort" to distinguish between revisionist states and states that initiated militarized action (1996, 178). Unfortunately, however, even a superhuman effort to do so seems destined to fail. The designation of disputants as revisionist or status-quo depends upon which state first "openly" challenges the existing order. However, because a very subtle and extended signaling process can precede any observable challenge to the status quo, the first state to issue such a challenge may not be the revisionist state in the conventional sense in which that term is understood.[8]

---

[7] A challenge can take the form of a territorial claim, an attempt to overthrow another government, or a refusal to comply with the foreign policy of another state (Jones, Bremer, and Singer 1996, 178).

[8] The issue of reputations can also make it difficult to separate revisionist and status-quo states. The accession to office of a government expected to challenge the status-quo can prompt its potential targets to act preemptively. That is, the reputation of a government as a revisionist state may make it the target of more challenges than status-quo

It is not surprising, then, that a great deal of overlap remains between the initiator and revisionist categories. In 76.5 percent of the MIDs in which the United States is involved between 1870 and 1992, it is coded as both the initiator and the revisionist state.[9] That the revisionist codings do not differ a great deal from the initiator codings suggests that the more recent MID data set should also carry the warning label that Small and Singer attach to their identification of initiators.

Therefore, I first examine the determinants of all U.S. MIDs and Max-MIDs between 1870 and 1992, without regard to whether the United States is identified as the revisionist or status-quo state. Then I analyze the determinants of only those disputes in which the United States is coded as the state which openly challenges the status quo. For the reasons just discussed, however, the results of this second set of analyses should be interpreted with caution.

Independent Variables

LEGISLATURES

This study involves one country in which an independent legislature has existed throughout the period under analysis. As a result, it is obviously impossible to observe any variations in the use of force as a function of changes in the basic structure of government. Thus, to assess the influence of an independent legislature, I use a dummy variable that takes on the value of one if the government is divided—that is, if the same party does not control both houses of Congress and the executive—and zero otherwise.

Divided government seems to be a reasonable proxy for an independent legislature for the following reason. The founding fathers lodged the power to declare war in Congress to check the executive's inclination to use force. The phenomenon of divided government is due to a similar but more general logic. Among students of American politics, split-ticket voting seems to many to reflect the desire of voters to achieve more moderate policy outcomes than a unified government would generate (Alesina and Rosenthal 1995; Cox 1990; Fiorina 1991).

To the extent that this objective is realized, it seems reasonable to expect that constraints on the president's use of force abroad will be tighter under divided than under unified governments.[10] Partisan con-

---

governments, washing out or even reversing the distinction between types (Gaubatz 1991; Smith 1996).

[9] I am grateful to Randolph M. Siverson for suggesting that I examine this issue.

[10] Analysts disagree about the consequences of divided government, in part because they

cerns about the next election may have the same effect. Because the majority of legislators in a unified government want the incumbent party to retain the White House, presidents in control of these governments are likely to be granted more latitude than are those who lead divided governments (Smith 1996, 148).

Between 1870 and 1992, divided governments were in office for 49 years (39.8 percent of the years in the sample). Of the 74 years in which unified governments held office, Democratic control prevailed for 38 (51.4 percent), and Republican control for 36 (48.6 percent). Of the 21 years after the onset of the Cold War in which unified governments prevailed, the Democrats controlled government for 18 years (85.7 percent), and the Republicans for 3 (14.3 percent).

ELECTIONS

To test whether the use of force varies within electoral cycles, I construct a dummy variable that takes on a value of one in presidential election years and zero otherwise. I also control for the state of the U.S. economy, because several studies find that a lagging economy increases presidential recourse to force abroad (e.g., Brace and Hinckley 1992; Hess and Orphanides 1995; James and Oneal 1991; Ostrom, Simon, and Job 1986).[11]

Some analysts suggest that the more general state of the world in which elections are held influences whether incumbents will make an effort to manipulate policy in order to affect electoral outcomes (e.g., Schultz 1995). Among the relevant elements is the incumbent's popular approval rating or his standing in preelection polls. Unfortunately, no data are available about either throughout the period studied here. Miller (1995), among others, however, suggests that a relatively high correlation exists between economic conditions and popular approval ratings. Thus, the former seems to be a reasonable proxy for the latter.

Among various macroeconomic indicators, the real GNP growth rate is widely recognized as the best summary measure of economic activity, (Alesina and Rosenthal 1995, 212). Moreover, it emerges as the most important economic variable in analyses of presidential elections (Fair 1978; 1988; 1996). Thus, I use real growth rates as a measure of the state of the economy and as a proxy for presidential popularity.

In his most recent work on presidential elections, Ray C. Fair uses the growth rate per capita of real GDP during the last three quarters of the

---

have yet to agree on how to measure its effects (Fiorina 1992; Mayhew 1991; McCubbins 1991).

[11] For example, Ostrom, Simon, and Job (1986) use a modified misery index and find that it is directly related to the incidence of U.S. disputes between 1948 and 1976.

election year. Because quarterly growth rates are not available before 1914, however, I use real annual growth rates here. I use Christina Romer's (1989) GNP data to compute these rates before 1914; thereafter I use the rates reported by the Statistical Abstract of the United States. I also use the growth-rate data to construct an interaction term that allows for a differential effect of the state of the economy during an election year. In the tables I label this interaction term "Elecgnp."

Control Variables: International Politics

Many students of international relations believe that domestic politics play a large role in determining foreign policy. Few, if any, however, maintain that politics abroad do not matter at all. For this reason, I control for the influence on U.S. recourse to force of systemic-level factors. In particular, I analyze the effects of variations in the level of U.S. national power and the advent of general wars.

Theory suggests and empirical studies confirm that major powers are much more likely than are other states to become involved in armed disputes, including war (e.g., Bremer 1992b). Small and Singer identify a small set of major powers across time, using various demographic, industrial, and military indicators (1982, 45). The United States enters this set as of 1898.

After World War II, Small and Singer define as major powers the permanent members of the U.N. Security Council (i.e., Britain, France, Taiwan/China, the Soviet Union, and the United States). Many other observers, however, believe that two superpowers populated the Cold War world: the United States and the Soviet Union (e.g., Powell 1996; Snyder 1984; Waltz 1979).[12]

Relative scores across time on a resource-based index support this belief. For example, in 1930 Britain and the United States receive almost identical scores; by 1960, however, the British score is only 25 percent of the U.S. score and 40 percent of the Soviet score (Ferris 1973, 56). For this reason I use three measures of national power: small, major, and superpower.[13]

To measure the effects of changes in these levels, I construct a set of

[12] Even Small and Singer (1982) are not completely comfortable with their post–World War II codings.

[13] This distinction is also useful because of the covariation between unified Democratic governments and the period in which the United States is a superpower. If the latter indeed has a positive effect on the dependent variable, omitting a control for superpower status would bias the coefficient on government structure.

dummy variables to indicate three different time periods: the 1870–97 period, when the United States is a small or "ordinary" power;[14] 1898–1949, when the United States is one of several major powers; and the Cold War years, when the United States becomes a superpower. Among the three, probably the most arbitrary demarcation is that for the initiation of the Cold War. Any year between 1945 and 1950 is reasonable. Here I use 1949, when the creation of the North Atlantic Treaty Organization made explicit the U.S. commitment to defend Western Europe.[15]

I also distinguish between periods in which general wars and other disputes occur. Although not universal, this distinction is common in the larger literature on war (e.g., Gilpin 1981; Levy 1983; Midlarsky 1988; Thompson 1985; 1993; cf. Bueno de Mesquita 1990). It is impossible to test whether general wars differ from other wars: only two general wars (World Wars I and II) occur during the sample period. As a result, whether to make this distinction depends upon the question at hand.

The United States did not enter either war until at least two years after each began, and, in the end, it had relatively little discretion about whether to do so. Of the seven wars the United States has entered since 1870, those that most closely approximate exogenous events are the world wars.[16] Since unified governments held office during both, omitting a control for them would bias downward the estimated effect of divided control of government. Thus, I construct a dummy variable that equals one for the world war periods (i.e., 1914–18 and 1939–45) and zero otherwise.

THE RESULTS

The dependent variable is the number of MIDs or MaxMIDs the United States enters each year between 1870 and 1992.[17] As the dependent variable is discrete and truncated at zero, an ordinary least squares (OLS)

[14] Rosecrance coined this term (1976, 11).

[15] Making the transition year any other year between 1945 and 1950 does not change any of the results reported below.

[16] These seven include, apart from the world wars themselves, the Spanish-American War, the Boxer Rebellion, the Korean War, the Vietnam War, and the Persian Gulf War.

[17] Because rally effects can be short-lived, I have also substituted for the dependent variable the number of MIDs and MaxMIDs that occur in August, September, and October of each year. There are only two differences. In the analysis of MIDs, the GNP growth rate is negative and significant (p-value < 0.047). In the analysis of MaxMIDs, the world war variable loses its significance. Complete results are available from the author.

regression will not generate efficient parameter estimates. The data conform most closely to a Poisson model, which is commonly used to model discrete count data that fit a Poisson distribution, as do the data here.[18] Thus, I use a Poisson model to test whether either or both the domestic political calendar and partisan politics influence the use of force abroad.

MIDS AND MAXMIDS, 1

In the first column of table 3.2, I report the results of an analysis of all MIDs. The second column reports the results of an analysis of Max-MIDs. The base group consists of unified government in a nonpresidential election year, during the period in which the United States is an ordinary power.

Regardless of whether the dependent variable is the annual number of all MIDs or only MaxMIDs, the results show that no coefficient on any variable related to political-military cycles or to the partisan composition of government is statistically significant.[19] In addition, the set of election-year variables is not jointly significant in either specification. Thus, the incidence of dispute engagements is unrelated to electoral cycles, and it is also independent of whether or not a unified government exists.

In contrast, two of the three control variables related to international politics exert significant effects. As table 3.2 shows, acquisition of major-power status does not have a statistically significant effect on the incidence of either set of MIDs. However, the onset of a world war exerts a positive and significant effect on the level of both MIDs (p-value = 0.001) and MaxMIDs (p-value < 0.0005), as does the advent of super-power status (p-value < 0.0005). The striking effects of these variables are graphically displayed in figure 3.1, which plots a three-year moving average of MIDs against time.

---

[18] That is, a χ^2 goodness-of-fit test fails to reject the null hypothesis that the data are Poisson distributed in each of the specifications presented below. In addition, fitting a negative binomial model shows no evidence of overdispersion, and a Lagrange Multiplier test fails to reject the null hypothesis of no serial correlation.

[19] Some suggest the use of force may be higher immediately after an election (e.g., Gaubatz 1991; Smith 1996). The results in this chapter do not change if I substitute for the election-year variable a dummy variable that codes whether a president is in the first two years of his term. Gaubatz's results, as he points out, may be a product of his reliance on bivariate analyses.

TABLE 3.2

Poisson Analysis of Number of U.S. MIDs: Electoral Cycles, Government Structure, and International Variables (Annual Data, 1870–1992)

	MIDs	MaxMIDs
Presidential election year	−0.2018	−0.3765
	(0.2044)	(0.4346)
GNP growth rate	−0.0234	−0.0221
	(0.0160)	(0.0263)
Elecgnp	0.0303	0.0972
	(0.0401)	(0.0757)
Divided government	0.0827	0.1358
	(0.1367)	(0.2698)
Major power	0.0140	0.8459
	(0.2650)	(0.5871)
Superpower	1.5023**	2.0309**
	(0.2108)	(0.5226)
World war	0.9299**	1.4953**
	(0.2716)	(0.3965)
Constant	−0.0540	−1.9871**
	(0.2185)	(0.5342)
Log L	−192.8	−118.7
N = 123		

Note: The numbers in parentheses are standard errors.   *$p < 0.05$, two-tailed test.   **$p < 0.01$, two-tailed test.

Because the superpower variable is a time-period dummy, however, its effects might be due to other, coterminous changes. Perhaps the most obvious candidate is the secular increase in the number of states, which also increased dispute opportunities. Membership in the international system rose from 55 in 1944 to 125 in 1970. This increase reflects, in part, the outcome of World War II, which allowed 13 states that Nazi Germany had occupied to reenter the system and which also led to the dis-

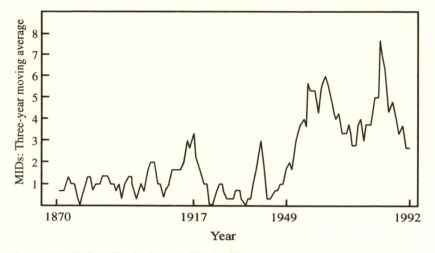

Figure 3.1. U.S. MIDs by Year, 1870–1992

mantling of the British and French colonial empires.[20] Thus, the postwar increase in U.S. MID rates may be the product of increasing dispute opportunities rather than of a change in U.S. power status.

If this were so, the number of disputes in the international system should be positively related to the number of member nations. However, the opposite is true: the number of MIDs is inversely related to the number of interstate system members (p-value = 0.065) (Jones, Bremer, and Singer 1996, 185). Thus, the post-1949 jump in U.S. involvement in disputes abroad cannot be attributed to an increase in system membership. It is, however, consistent with the established finding that major powers are more likely to become involved in disputes abroad.

MIDS AND MAXMIDS, 2

In this section, I analyze the likelihood of disputes in which the United States is coded as the revisionist state. This includes 95 of the 262 disputes

[20] According to Waltz (1979), only four states (Estonia, Latvia, Lithuania, and Tibet) met "involuntary ends" in the half-century prior to 1979. Thus, he concludes, the death rate of states is small. However, using Waltz's implicit measure (i.e., the occupation of states), calculations based on COW data show a much higher death rate: between 1929 and 1979, 22 states die. During the 120 years in the sample period, 38 states die: 9 between 1870 and 1913; 5 between 1914 and 1938; 14 between 1939 and 1944; and another 10 thereafter. However, since many of these states later reentered the system, including three members of Waltz's set, it might be more accurate to describe states as comatose rather than dead.

39

in which the United States is involved between 1870 and 1992 (Jones, Bremer, and Singer 1996). Of the 95 MIDs that involve a U.S. challenge, 54 are either threats to use or displays of force, and 41 are either uses of force or war. As might be expected, the mean number of revisionist MIDs is significantly larger during the Cold War than it is earlier.

As before, the base group consists of unified government in a nonpresidential election year, during the period in which the United States is an ordinary power. Table 3.3 reports the results of an analysis of all MIDs and MaxMIDs in which the United States is reported to have challenged the status quo.[21]

The results in table 3.3 are generally consistent with those for all MIDs and MaxMIDs. They show that no coefficient on any variable related to political-military cycles is significant in either specification.[22] Nor are these variables jointly significant. Although the transition to major-power status does not have any significant effect,[23] the coefficient on the world war variable in the MaxMIDs case and that on the superpower variable in both cases remain positive and significant.

The one difference that does emerge involves the effect of government structure. The results of the analyses of MIDs and MaxMIDs in general showed that no variable related to the partisan composition of government had a statistically significant effect on dispute involvements. Table 3.3 shows, however, that divided governments are more likely to challenge the status quo than are unified governments in the case of revisionist MIDs (p-value = 0.032). This is, of course, inconsistent with the prediction that divided government reduces recourse to force abroad.

CONCLUSION

In the analyses in this chapter, the advent of superpower status and the outbreak of world wars emerge as the most consistent and statistically significant determinants of U.S. dispute rates across the sets and levels of

[21] Substituting as before for the dependent variable the number of MIDs and MaxMIDs that occur in August, September, and October of each year, the coefficient on GNP growth is negative and significant for all revisionist MIDs, while the coefficient on the world war variable is insignificant. In the analysis of revisionist MaxMIDs, none of the variables is significant. Complete results are available from the author.

[22] Nor is a variable that controls for whether a government is in the first two years of its term in office. See n. 19 above.

[23] The coefficient on the major-power variable in the case of revisionist MaxMIDs is marginally significant (p-value = 0.064).

TABLE 3.3

Poisson Analysis of Number of U.S. Revisionist MIDs: Electoral Cycles, Government Structure, and International Variables (Annual Data, 1870–1992)

	MIDs	*MaxMIDs*
Presidential election year	− 0.3090	− 0.4749
	(0.3005)	(0.5774)
GNP growth rate	− 0.0110	− 0.0442
	(0.0242)	(0.0335)
Elecgnp	− 0.0110	0.1100
	(0.0539)	(0.1000)
Divided government	0.5189*	0.5600
	(0.2420)	(0.3879)
Major power	0.5278	1.9894
	(0.3873)	(1.0731)
Superpower	1.1358	2.7521**
	(0.3329)	(1.0222)
World war	0.7211	1.5204**
	(0.3923)	(0.5163)
Constant	− 1.1754**	− 3.5952**
	(0.3540)	(1.0416)
Log L	− 132.03	− 79.86
N = 123		

Note: The numbers in parentheses are standard errors. *p < 0.05, two-tailed test. **p < 0.01, two-tailed test.

disputes analyzed. The use of force abroad is invariant to the domestic political calendar; that is, the advent of a presidential election year does not have any observable effect on the incidence of U.S. engagement in armed disputes abroad, regardless of the level of the dispute.

The invariance of disputes to the electoral cycle is inconsistent with findings in the "rally-round-the-flag" literature. It is, however, consistent with the checks-and-balance interpretation. This consistency may be the product of the same factors that explain why political-business cycles are rarely observed (see, e.g., Lucas 1972; Sargent and Wallace 1975). That is, explicit attention to the logic of rational expectations makes clear that any effort to use military power abroad to wage political battles at home will be futile: nonmyopic voters will discount the use of force as elections approach; as a result, nonmyopic leaders will not attempt to use this instrument to influence votes.

The analyses in this chapter also show that recourse to force does not vary consistently with the partisan composition of government. Whether or not a unified government exists matters in only instance—in the case of MIDs in which the United States initiates a challenge to the status quo. The problems that plague efforts to distinguish between revisionist and status-quo states, as well as the sensitivity of the partisan result to the definition of disputes, however, make this finding somewhat tenuous.

That the composition of government does not exert a stronger and more consistent imprint on U.S. recourse to force is at odds with the predictions of the democratic-peace literature, particularly in light of evidence that the parties' preferences on foreign-policy diverge (Poole and Rosenthal 1991). This apparent puzzle might have a simple solution: unlike decisions about trade, for example, decisions about using force tend to be exigent responses to international events.

However, because it has long been either a major power or a superpower, the United States has had a great deal of discretion about whether and when to use force to respond to events abroad. Partisan politics has nevertheless remained largely muted. Indeed, the celebrated bipartisanship with respect to foreign policy that many believe characterized the early Cold War period seems to have prevailed for more than a century. As chapter 2 noted, this may be the product of the relatively weak incentives of legislators to enter the policy process when the issue at stake involves the use of force abroad.

Another possibility is that the parties themselves may be better off if they conclude a tacit partisan truce with respect to the use of military power. As I have discussed at greater length elsewhere (Gowa 1998), doing so can enable the parties to maximize their own rather than social welfare. In this interpretation, adherence to a tacit truce is a means to escape rather than a reflection of accountability. If this is correct, it suggests a subversion of a checks-and-balance system. As a consequence, it dilutes the power of the structural-constraints explanation of the democratic peace.

On the whole, then, the analyses in this chapter and in the preceding one suggest that the democratic-peace hypothesis rests upon weak microfoundations. This implies, in turn, that the empirical support for it may also be weaker than the existing literature depicts it to be. The next chapter, therefore, examines the relative incidence of disputes between members of democratic dyads and those of other country pairs.

Reinterpreting the Democratic Peace

WITH HENRY FARBER

THE RESULTS of the analyses of dispute-rate data presented in this chapter differ markedly from those in the existing literature. They show that war and other militarized disputes between democratic states are relatively rare only during the Cold War. Between 1816 and 1914, members of pairs of democratic states are no less likely to engage each other in war or in other militarized disputes than are their nondemocratic counterparts.

The first section describes the data and research design used to reexamine the empirical foundations of the democratic-peace hypothesis. The results of the empirical analyses are then presented and discussed.

RESEARCH DESIGN

The Sample

As noted in chapter 1, not all contributors to debates about the democratic peace operationalize their dependent variable in exactly the same way. Some include both wars and armed disputes short of war, because they interpret peaceful conflict resolution as precluding any recourse to arms (e.g., Bremer 1993; Maoz and Abdolali 1989; Maoz and Russett 1993; Morgan and Campbell 1991; Morgan and Schwebach 1992; Russett 1995). Others, however, believe that only full-scale war is relevant (e.g., Chan 1984; Lake 1992; Ray 1993; Spiro 1994). Driving this largely implicit debate about which conflicts are appropriate to test the democratic-peace hypothesis is a disagreement about the definition of "peaceful" conflict resolution.

The analytic foundations of the democratic-peace hypothesis seem to dictate the inclusion of all armed disputes. For example, the norm-based explanation posits that if a conflict of interests arises between two democratic polities, it will be settled without recourse to violence, because of the externalization of domestic norms mandating peaceful conflict resolution. This implies that democratic states will forgo recourse to force at any level in the event of a dispute between them.[1]

More generally, the distinction between cheap talk and credible threats supports the inclusion of even the lowest-level MIDs, that is, a threat to use military force. If a threat takes the form of cheap talk, the target nation has no more incentive to settle a conflict than if no threat at all had been issued.[2] Only if a threat takes the form of a costly signal will the probability of a negotiated settlement increase. That is, if a threat "risks or costs nothing," as James D. Fearon observes, it "conveys no information [about a nation's resolve] and should not rationally lead the target state to change its beliefs" (1992, 40–41). As such, credible threats to use force signal that a state is prepared to invoke military power, if necessary, to settle a dispute. This makes the universe of MIDs relevant to a test of whether peaceful conflict resolution is more likely in cases of disputes between two democracies than in other cases.

For these reasons, the analyses in this chapter examine wars alone, as well as armed disputes short of war, to establish whether relations between democratic polities are uniquely peaceful.[3]

War

As is standard, the definition and measurement of interstate wars in the analyses that follow come from the Correlates of War (COW) data set (Small and Singer 1982).[4] Thus, a war is defined as a clash that involves "one or more system members" and that leads "to a minimum of 1,000 battle fatalities among all of the system members involved." The definitions of system members and belligerents also follow that of the COW project (Small and Singer 1982, 155).[5]

---

[1] This, in turn, suggests that whether disputes between democracies escalate to war as often as do those between nondemocracies is an interesting issue in its own right, but it is not a substitute for the question of whether a democratic peace exists. For an analysis of the issue of dispute escalation, see Senese (1997).

[2] Fearon defines cheap talk as "statements or actions that are costless to make or that carry the same costs regardless of the sender's true intent" (1992, 5).

[3] With one exception (see chapter 6, n.4), the sign and significance of the joint-democracy variable do not change if both wars and disputes are analyzed together.

[4] These data are taken directly from the public-use version of the COW war data set (part 1 of ICPSR Study Number 9044).

[5] That is, a nation is a member of the interstate system before 1914 if and only if (1) it had a minimum population of 500,000, and (2) it had British and French representation on its soil "at or above the rank of charge d'affaires." After World War I, a nation so qualified if

As is also standard in the literature, a dyad-year is used as the unit of observation: that is, the unit of observation is a record of whether or not a dispute or war occurs between the members of each pair of countries during each year in the sample. The requisite data are available for the 1816–1980 period. Thus, the basic sample consists of 307,322 dyad-years.[6] That war is a rare event is clear: the sample contains 856 dyad-years (0.28 percent) at war, distributed across 67 interstate wars.

Three modifications are made to the standard use of the war data set in the democratic-peace literature. The first change relates to the convention in the democratic-peace literature of coding all 856 dyad-years as warring observations (see, e.g., Chan 1984, 621). Doing so treats the onset and the continuation of wars between countries identically. Given that the issue of central importance is the incidence, rather than the duration, of war, it seems more sensible to count each war between the members of a pair of states as only a single warring observation.

The use of only a single observation partially solves a related statistical issue. Including all observations for a given dyad within the same war effectively means that these observations are treated as independent despite the fact that they are not. Statistical inferences using measures based on the assumption of independence are likely to be misleading, however. The problem is particularly acute in the case at hand: war is such a rare event that treating successive warring dyad-years as independent observations greatly overstates the incidence of war.[7]

As a result, a more restrictive measure is used here. A war outcome is coded as such only the first year a dyad is involved in a particular war. All

---

it was (1) "a member of the League of Nations or the United Nations at any time during its existence," or (2) it "met the half million population requirement and received diplomatic missions from *any two* . . . major powers" (Small and Singer 1982, 40–41, emphasis in original). Small and Singer classify a state as a belligerent in a war if it either committed one thousand troops to battle or suffered at least one hundred casualties (1982, 55).

[6] By including every possible dyad-year for which complete data exist on both members, many dyad-years are included whose members are very unlikely to have meaningful contact of any kind, let alone have a military dispute. One approach, used by Maoz and Russett (1993), is to include only dyad-years whose members are contiguous or have at least one major power as a member. While it is true that noncontiguous dyad-years with no major powers have much lower dispute rates, there are more than a few disputes involving such dyad-years. Thus, all dyad-years and controls for contiguity and major-power status are included here. All of the analyses in this study have been repeated using the restricted sample of dyad-years, and the results are qualitatively identical.

[7] Of course, a similar lack of independence characterizes successive observations for a dyad at peace. This problem is discussed below.

subsequent years the dyad is involved in the same war are deleted from the sample. The years in which a dyad is at peace are coded as nonwar observations. For example, the less restrictive measure records the 1877–78 war between Russia and Turkey as two dyad-years at war. The measure used here records the war as only one dyad-year at war (1877), and it excludes from the analysis the remaining dyad-year (1878). The reduced sample based on this measure contains 306,770 dyad-years, of which 304 are dyad-years at war (0.10 percent).

A second modification to the use of the standard data set involves distinguishing between general and other wars. This conforms to the practice of many, although not all, students of war, as noted in the preceding chapter. Whether this distinction makes sense depends, as before, upon the specific issue at hand. Here, the issue is whether members of pairs of democratic nations are less likely to wage war against each other than are members of other pairs of states; that is, it is interactions within dyads that are of central concern.

The dynamics of general wars, however, render a dyad a substantively meaningless unit of observation. A dyad-based measure cannot capture the attempts to "pass the buck" that dominated the periods immediately before both World War I and World War II.[8] These attempts are crucial to explaining the outbreak of both wars, however: in their absence, deterrence might have succeeded. Nor can measures based on dyads capture the evolution of general wars. States did not enter World War I and World War II as discrete pairs. As a result, it is not theories and measures based on dyads but theories and measures based on the diffusion of war that are relevant in the context of the prosecution of these wars (see, e.g., Siverson and Starr 1991).

Thus, with one exception, the periods that include the world wars (1914–18 and 1939–45) are dropped from the empirical analyses that follow.[9] Note that this is not a trivial change. These two periods contain not only both world wars (498 dyad-years at war) but also three small

[8] See Posen (1984) for an incisive account of buck-passing in the interwar period.

[9] While not a perfect solution to the problem of how to examine only nongeneral wars, dropping the time periods of the great wars is superior to dropping only those dyad-years fighting in the great wars. It is not appropriate to drop a dyad-year simply because that specific dyad was fighting a war in that year. Such a sample-selection rule would run a serious risk of introducing sample-selection bias. The decision to drop the time periods of the two world wars drops many more observations not at war (11,851) than observations at war, so that any sample-selection bias induced by dropping these periods is likely to be much less serious than deleting only dyad-years at war.

47

wars (eight dyad-years at war). The two periods together make up only 5.1 percent of the dyad-years in the sample, but they account for fully 59.1 percent of the dyad-years at war (506 of 856). Indeed, that over half (58.2 percent) of the warring observations are in the world wars itself suggests that these wars differ from others.

Finally, with the exception of the world wars, all belligerents and all wars that Small and Singer code are included in the analysis. In particular, the sample used in the first analysis includes the World War II dyads in which Finland is a member. Some analysts purge these dyads from their data. The effect of doing so is to undercount the number of wars that have occurred between democratic polities.

The exclusion of the Finnish observations makes some sense. Finland was a belligerent against the Western allies during World War II in name only: it engaged only Soviet troops in battle during that war (Russett 1993, 18). However, a reclassification of cases is appropriate if and only if it is based upon the application of the redefined standard to all entries in the relevant data sets.[10] In the case at hand, for example, dropping the Finnish dyads would not create a potential for biased inferences if all other similar cases were also dropped (i.e., those cases in which a member of a wartime alliance did not attack all the member states of the opposing alliance). As the democratic-peace literature stands, however, the omission of the Finnish dyads biases the results in favor of the finding that disputes between democracies are relatively rare events. Thus, Finland is coded here as a belligerent in the Second World War.

Lower-Level MIDs

As in the case of wars, COW data are used to measure militarized interstate disputes.[11] In contrast to chapter 2, this chapter uses data from the original MID data set. It does so to ensure that the analyses here provide a straightforward comparison to existing studies of the democratic peace.

As noted in the preceding chapter, an international event classifies as a MID if it involves "government-sanctioned" "threats to use military force, displays of military force, . . . actual uses of force," or war (Gochman and Maoz 1984, 587). The original data set records the occurrence

---

[10] Despite his ad hoc exclusion of some wars, Ray acknowledges this problem (1993, 269). Bremer (1992b) also recognizes it.

[11] These data are taken directly from the public-use version of the COW militarized interstate dispute data set (part 3 of ICPSR Study Number 9044). Gochman and Maoz (1984) describe the MID data in more detail.

of 837 disputes from 1817 through 1976, excluding the periods of the world wars.

Using the MID data, a variable is constructed which indicates for each dyad-year in the sample whether or not the two countries in that dyad were on opposite sides of at least one dispute in that year.[12] In the sample are 2,710 dyad-years with disputes, representing 1,550 initial years of disputes. These initial years constitute 0.51 percent of the 306,162 dyad-years from 1817 through 1976. Subsequent years of a dispute are coded as missing.

For each country involved in any given MID, Small and Singer record the most severe hostility level reached among four possible levels: (1) threat to use force, (2) display of force, (3) use of force, and (4) outbreak of a Small-Singer war. To measure the level of hostility focused on the opposing member of the dyad, the level of hostility of each member of a disputing dyad is recorded. Coded as lower-level MIDs are all disputes where neither member of a dyad is recorded as having a level of hostility equal to a Small-Singer war.[13] Of the 1,550 disputing dyads, 1,246 are coded as having lower-level disputes.[14]

Polity Type

The analyses below use Ted Robert Gurr's Polity II data set to define autocratic, democratic, and anocratic regimes, as is standard.[15] Gurr defines autocracies as systems in which (1) tight constraints on political participation exist, (2) only members of the political elite select the chief executive, and (3) institutions do not constrain the leader's power. In

---

[12] There are cases where two countries are involved in more than one dispute with each other in a particular year.

[13] In fact, the MID data code only the maximum level of hostility reached by each participant considered individually. This makes it is impossible to determine the hostility level reached between specific pairs of countries in a multilateral dispute. Where there is more than one dispute involving a specific dyad in a given year, we code the level of hostility of each side as the maximum level of hostility reached by that side in any dispute involving both members of the dyad that year.

[14] Fully 422 of these dyads are potentially miscoded because data on the level of hostility are missing for at least one dyad member. However, because none of these 422 dyad-years are listed in the COW war data, it is unlikely that there are substantial numbers of warring dyads included in our lower-level disputing dyad sample.

[15] ICPSR Study Number 9263. Some studies also use an additional data set to assess polity types (e.g., Banks 1971; Chan 1984). See, e.g., Bremer (1992b); Maoz and Russett (1993).

contrast, in democracies (1) individuals can "express effective preferences about alternative policies and leaders," (2) institutionalized constraints limit the leader's power, and (3) guarantees of civil liberties exist (Gurr 1990, 37–38).

Gurr constructs two discrete 10-point scales to measure the extent of autocracy and democracy in each state annually.[16] The scores a polity receives are composite measures that reflect, inter alia, the method of executive recruitment, the competitiveness of party politics, and the range of political participation. Gurr labels as "anocratic" those polities that receive "middling scores on both Autocracy and Democracy scales" (1990, 38).[17]

Using Gurr's scales, each polity is categorized as democratic, autocratic, or anocratic. More specifically, a polity is categorized as democratic if it receives a score of six or more on Gurr's democracy scale, as autocratic if it scores five or higher on Gurr's autocracy scale, and as anocratic if it is categorized as neither a democracy nor an autocracy.[18]

According to this criterion, Spain classifies as a democracy in 1898, making the Spanish-American War a war between democratic polities. Many contributors to the democratic-peace literature recode Spain as nondemocratic, thereby transforming the 1898 war into a war between nondemocracies. As in the Finnish case, this reclassification makes some sense. A plausible case can be made that Spain was not "really" democratic in 1898 (see, e.g., Ray 1993, 264). As was also true of the Finnish dyads, however, the danger of potentially biased inferences exists, because this redefinition has not been applied to all other cases in the Polity data set. In the analyses that follow, therefore, Spain is coded on the basis

[16] There are three types of cases which Gurr codes as missing. "Interruptions" are cases in which a wartime occupation temporarily disrupts an existing polity. The other two cases are "transitions," defined as periods of change from one regime type to another, and "interregnums," defined as periods during which no central government exists. These cases are coded here as nondemocracies; doing otherwise would omit five wars from the pre-1914 sample.

[17] More intuitively, an anocracy describes a polity in which the state exercises very limited power, no institutionalized pattern of political competition exists, and leaders are in constant peril of being overthrown. Anocracy "means literally the absence of power or control," although it is used "to signify states which approach but do not reach the extreme conditions" (Gurr 1974, 1487, n.11).

[18] These rules do not generate any inconsistencies. Specifically, there are no regimes that satisfy both the requirement for a democracy and the requirement for an autocracy. The simple correlation between Gurr's autocracy and democracy scales is −0.83.

of the Gurr ranking, making the Spanish-American War a war between democratic states.

Control Variables

Theoretical studies and empirical analyses suggest that a number of variables other than polity type influence the probability of war and other militarized disputes. Thus, analyses of the democratic peace often include major-power status, contiguity, national wealth, and interests as control variables.

Major-power status strongly affects dispute probabilities (Bremer 1992b). Thus, it is included as a control variable here. On the basis of Small and Singer's (1982) classification of major powers, the number of major powers in each dyad (0, 1, or 2) is recorded. As is standard in the democratic-peace literature, a pair of dummy variables indicates whether a dyad includes one or two major powers.[19]

Whether two states are contiguous also is known to influence the probability that they will become involved in a war or other militarized dispute. To construct a measure of it, Siverson and Starr's border data (1991), extended through 1980, are used. Members of a dyad can be contiguous in one or more of three ways: they can share home or colonial borders, or they can be separated by less than two hundred miles of water. If they are not contiguous in any of these ways, they are classified as noncontiguous. In the probit model, a single dummy variable indicates whether or not dyad members are contiguous.[20]

Neither wealth nor interests are used as regressors. The lack of data explains the omission of wealth. Consistent and reliable measures of gross national product for the countries in the sample are not available before World War II. This, of course, creates a potential omitted-variable problem; that is, if the included and omitted variables are correlated, the parameter estimates will be biased. The direction of the bias takes the sign of the product of (1) the correlation between the included and omitted

---

[19] No separate dummy is used to indicate superpower status, because, unlike in the last chapter, no risk exists of confounding the effects of two independent variables.

[20] Siverson and Starr record as an event additions and removals of a boundary of a given type, but they do not record whether all boundaries of a given type are removed when a removal is recorded. Thus, possible inaccuracies are inherent in these data if, after the last recorded removal of a boundary of a given type (e.g., colonial), existing boundaries of that type remain.

variables and (2) the expected regression coefficient on the omitted variable.

In the case at hand, a positive correlation exists between democratic polities and national wealth (see, e.g., Bollen 1979; 1983; Bollen and Jackman 1985; Burkhart and Lewis-Beck 1994; Londregan and Poole 1996).[21] Empirical analyses of the post–World War II period also show that an inverse relationship exists between the national wealth of members of a dyad and the probability of a MID between them (Maoz and Russett 1993, 632). As a result, omitting a control for wealth seems likely to bias downward the coefficient on the democracy variable.[22] In other words, the absence of a measure of national output decreases the coefficient on the democracy variable in tests of the democratic-peace hypothesis. Thus, empirical analyses that do not control for national wealth are biased in favor of finding support for the existence of a democratic peace.

A measure of interests is not included in the analyses for a different reason. Alliances are often used to proxy common interests in multivariate models of dispute propensities, because no more direct measure of interests exists or can be constructed (Bueno de Mesquita 1981; Bueno de Mesquita and Lalman 1992; Dixon 1994; Siverson and Emmons 1991; Siverson and Starr 1991). Doing so creates severe inference problems, however, because of a simultaneity problem: alliances are the outcome of current and expected future strategic interactions among states, including either actual or nascent disputes.

To illustrate, suppose that a simple model of disputes that allows for the effect of polity type could be based on an underlying score measuring the propensity of the members of a dyad to engage each other in MIDs. Define this score for a pair of countries i and j in year t as

$$Y_{ijt} = \beta_1 Int_{ijt} + \beta_2 Dem_{ijt} + X_{ijt}\beta_3 + \epsilon_{ijt}, \tag{1}$$

where Y is the dispute propensity, Int is a variable measuring the degree to which states i and j have interests in common, Dem is a dummy variable indicating whether or not both countries in the dyad are democratic, X is a vector of other explanatory variables, ϵ is a random component,

---

[21] Whether the correlation reflects a causal link has been the subject of a long debate in political science. For recent analyses, see Burkhart and Lewis-Beck (1994); Londregan and Poole (1996).

[22] This applies, of course, if and only if the relationships between democracy and wealth and between wealth and disputes are of constant sign across the 1816–1980 period.

and the β's are parameters to be estimated. A standard approach to estimation of this model would be to assume that a dispute is observed between countries i and j in year t if and only if $Y_{ijt} > 0$ and to assume that the random component has a particular convenient distribution.[23]

The central claim of the democratic peace literature is that $\beta_2 < 0$; that is, democratic dyads are less likely to fight. The standard assumption in this literature and in the international relations literature more generally is that $\beta_1 < 0$; that is, the more common interests members of country pairs share, the lower is their dispute propensity.

A reasonable empirical model of alliances has a similar structure. Define an underlying score measuring the propensity of the members of a dyad, i and j, to ally with each other in year t as

$$W_{ijt} = \delta_1 \text{Int}_{ijt} + \delta_2 \text{Dem}_{ijt} + Z_{ijt}\delta_3 + \mu_{ijt}, \qquad (2)$$

where W is the propensity to ally, Z is a vector of other explanatory variables, μ is a random component, and the δ's are parameters to be estimated. As in the case of disputes, the standard approach to estimation would be to assume that an alliance is observed between countries i and j in year t if and only if $W_{ijt} > 0$ and to assume that the random component has a particular convenient distribution. Presumably, δ_1 is positive, because dyads with interests in common are more likely to ally.

However reasonable it may seem, this approach introduces a serious simultaneity problem. To see this, assume that the propensity scores (Y and W) are observable. Then, if measures of all the variables were available, ordinary least squares (OLS) could be used to estimate equations (1) and (2). If the alliance propensity (W) proxies for interests (Int) in the dispute propensity equation, the estimating function takes the form

$$Y_{ijt} = \alpha_1 W_{ijt} + \alpha_2 \text{Dem}_{ijt} + X_{ijt}\alpha_3 + \theta_{ijt}. \qquad (3)$$

Aside from the use of a probit model and the use of alliances as a discrete measure of the propensity to ally (W), this is representative of existing analyses.

Whether it is reasonable to use this equation to estimate the effect of democracy on disputes depends in part upon how the α's map into the β's in equation (1). This is a problem, however, if the effect of democracy

---

[23] For example, if the distribution is assumed normal, then the result is a probit model. If the distribution is assumed extreme-value, then the result is a logit model.

on the propensity to ally controlling for interests (δ_2) is nonzero.[24] Of more consequence is the fact that, by construction, the alliance measure in equation (3) is positively correlated with the error term (θ).[25] This is so because disputes and alliances are both outcomes of interstate interactions (King, Keohane, and Verba 1994, 198). The result is biased and inconsistent parameter estimates throughout.

The sign of the bias in the estimate of the key parameter, the effect of democracy on dispute rates depends in an important way on the correlation of democracy with the propensity to ally. If the correlation is positive, the bias will be negative. If the correlation is negative, then the bias will be positive. Thus, including alliances in multivariate analyses of dispute propensities can lead to misleading estimates of the structural relationship between democracy and disputes.

For these reasons, the dispute propensity function without alliances or an alternative measure of interests is first estimated. This is a reduced form of the dispute propensity function with an important omitted variable, and the results need to be interpreted in this context. This issue and that of interests are addressed in more detail in succeeding chapters.

Disaggregating the Data

In order to verify that the data yield results consistent with those of previous studies, the entire 1816–1980 period, including the periods of the two world wars, is examined first. Thereafter, the data are disaggregated into three periods: pre–World War I (1816–1913), the interwar period, and post–World War II (1946–80). Although the analyses examine each

---

[24] Solving equation (2) for Int and substituting into equation (1) yields a relationship with the same form as equation (3). The coefficient on the democracy variable in this relationship is $\alpha_2 = \beta_2 + \beta_1\delta_2/\delta_1$. Thus, if $\delta_2 = 0$ then $\alpha_2 = \beta_2$. Whether $\delta_2 = 0$ or not depends on whether democracies are differentially likely to ally controlling for interests. No a priori reason for such a relationship is apparent, but the same rationale used to motivate the democratic peace could be used to motivate higher alliance rates between democracies conditional on interests ($\delta_2 > 0$).

[25] Once again, the relationship is derived by solving equation (2) for Int and substituting into equation (1). The error term in this relationship is $\theta_{ijt} = \epsilon_{ijt} - (\beta_1/\delta_1)\mu_{ijt}$. Since β_1 is presumably negative (reflecting lower disputes rates where there are more interests in common) and δ_1 is presumably positive (reflecting higher alliance rates where there are more interests in common) and since alliances are positively correlated with μ_{ijt} by construction (equation 2), the correlation between the alliance measure and the error term in equation (3) will be positive. Additionally, the error in the dispute equation (ϵ) may be correlated with alliances.

of these three periods, particular emphasis is placed on the pre-1914 and post-1945 periods. Three factors motivate these choices.

First, analytical and empirical studies establish that the pre–World War I and the post–World War II international systems differ in important ways. Theorists point to the advent in the later period of bipolarity (e.g., Waltz 1979) and nuclear weapons (e.g., Gaddis 1986). Empiricists point to differences between the centuries in such central processes as alliance formation and the outbreak of war (e.g., Chan 1993, 210; Duncan and Siverson 1982; Li and Thompson 1976; McGowan and Rood 1975). As discussed in more detail later, these differences have significant implications for the democratic peace.

Second, the post–World War II period dominates analyses of the entire period. Although the Cold War includes only about one-fifth (20.6 percent) of the years examined, it includes almost two-thirds (65 percent) of the dyad-years in the sample. Thus, Cold War observations swamp analyses of the 1816–1980 period as a whole. To the extent that the Cold War world differs from its predecessors, an aggregate analysis will yield a very misleading picture of the entire 1816–1980 period.

Disaggregating the data creates relatively small samples for the pre–World War II periods. This reduces the likelihood of finding statistically significant differences between pairs of democratic states and other country pairs. This risk is assumed because doing otherwise threatens to obscure variations in the relationship between polity types and dispute rates over time. A key feature of the analysis here is that it uses variations in the structure of the international system across time to help distinguish between a "pure" effect of democracy on dispute rates and an effect of democracy due to other factors (e.g., common or conflicting interests). As it turns out, dispute-rate patterns vary across the pre-1914 and post-1945 periods, providing important evidence about the democratic peace.

The decision to emphasize these two periods relative to the years between 1919 and 1938 follows from the fact that the interwar years do not form a discrete international system but are instead an interregnum between two very different systems. After World War I, serious major-power conflicts of interest about, for example, the future of Germany made it impossible to reconstruct a stable international system. As a result, the two decades that followed the signing of the Treaty of Versailles became simply a prelude to another world war. Thus, although the results of analyses of the interwar period are reported, they contribute less to the interpretation of dyadic dispute patterns than do the years before 1914 and those after 1945.

55

Methodological Issues

THE ASSUMPTION OF INDEPENDENCE

Most analysts use a standard probit or logit model to test whether democracies engage each other in armed conflicts at a lower rate than do members of other country pairs (e.g., Farber and Gowa 1995; 1997; Maoz and Russett 1993; Oneal and Russett 1997). These models assume that successive observations of a given dyad are independent. As in the case of multiyear wars and disputes discussed earlier, however, it seems more likely that temporal dependence characterizes succeeding observations of peace between members of any given country pair.

As noted, models like probit or logit rely on an unobservable latent variable (Y_{it}) to determine whether a conflict occurs between members of dyad i in year t. There is a conflict if Y_{it} is positive and there is no conflict otherwise. Let

$$Y_{it} = X_{it}\beta + \epsilon_{it}, \tag{4}$$

where ϵ_{it} is a random component, and the β's are parameters to be estimated. Assuming that ϵ has a normal distribution implies a probit model while assuming that ϵ has an extreme-value distribution implies a logit model.

A key assumption of these models is that the ϵ's are independent both across dyads and over time within dyads. This may not be a good assumption in this context for any of several reasons. The first involves the problem of heterogeneity. Persistent differences across dyads in their dispute propensities may exist that are not captured by the measured variables (contiguity, major power status, polity type). One approach to modeling this would be to estimate an error-components model of the form

$$Y_{it} = X_{it}\beta + \gamma_i + \epsilon_{it}, \tag{5}$$

where the γ's represent the unmeasured dyad-specific factors. There are two common ways to estimate this type of model.

The fixed-effect approach estimates the γ's explicitly as parameters of the model. This technique then relies on within-dyad variation in the X's to estimate the parameters of interest as the γ's "soak up" the between-dyad differences in conflict rates. In the context of the democratic peace, however, using this model is problematic. Because conflicts are so rare and because the central variable of interest, polity type, does not show much within-dyad variation, this approach results in using only a small fraction of the information in the data. In fact, observations on dyads that show no variation in the outcome (i.e., those that never had any conflicts) are effectively dropped from the analysis.

The other approach, the random-effects approach, does not actually involve estimation of the individual γ's. Instead, a distribution for the γ's is assumed and integrated out of an appropriately modified likelihood function. In the case at hand, if the ϵ's and the γ's are assumed to be independently and normally distributed, a random-effects probit model with normal error components can be estimated by adding only a single parameter (the variance of the distribution of the γ's) to the model. This parameter indicates how much persistent variation exists in dispute propensities across dyads after controlling for the observables. A weakness of the random-effects approach is that the results are likely to be sensitive to the distribution assumed for the γ's.

Another reason to be wary of the independence assumption that underlies standard probit or logit models is the possibility of serial correlation in the error term (the ϵ's). That is, unobservable shocks to the dispute-propensity function might persist for some period of time, creating a correlation across successive observations. This problem is very difficult to deal with in latent-variable models because the errors are never, in fact, observed.

The potential for state dependence is the third reason to worry about the use of these models. In other words, the dispute propensity might, in fact, depend on the time that has passed since the last dispute (i.e., the length of the most recent peace spell). As Beck, Katz, and Tucker (1997) correctly point out, state dependence can lead to biased estimates. Demonstrating that a model of dyadic conflict with state dependence can be usefully thought of as an event-history or duration model, they develop a straightforward generalization of the standard logit model that solves this problem by including controls for the length of the dyadic peace spell in progress at the start of any year.

In practice, adopting any of these alternative models encounters two competing problems. First, heterogeneity, serial correlation, and state dependence are very difficult to distinguish in practice. The discrete nature of the dependent variables exacerbates this identification problem, because information exists only about the sign but not about the actual value of the latent variable. Absent a very large amount of information (in the form of a large number of long time series), the observed time-series properties of even continuous variables in each of these three models can look very similar. Second, disputes are very rare, and the outcome measures and key explanatory variables show very little within-dyad variation. In sum, there is only so much information in the data, and allowing for a complicated error structure simply overtaxes the available information.

The Beck, Katz, and Tucker (1997) solution to the problem of state dependence is not appropriate if there is heterogeneity across dyads. Heterogeneity will yield what appears to be strong state dependence even when no true state dependence exists. Dyads that have very low dispute propensities will be disproportionately represented among dyad-years with long prior peace spells. As a result, it will not be surprising to find that dyad-years with long prior peace spells have low dispute propensities. This need not be the result of the long peace spell, however. It may reflect instead the unmeasured low dispute propensity of those dyads. As such, including the length of the peace spell is equivalent to including a lagged dependent variable in a model with correlated errors, and the result will be biased parameter estimates.

Given the limited information in the data and the lack of a clearly superior econometric approach, the results presented in the tables here are based on a standard probit model. Using this model reflects the information in the data with the least amount of filtering. Yet, the assumption of independence across observations makes it likely that the precision of the estimates obtained will be exaggerated. Thus, random-effects models controlling for heterogeneity and event-history models of the reported dispute propensities were also estimated. While the results are not presented here, the estimates, with one exception noted below, confirm the conclusions of the standard analysis.[26]

EMPTY-MARGIN PROBLEMS

The analysis of wars poses yet another complication. Although lower-level MIDs are quite rare, wars are rarer still. Between the wars and after World War II, no wars occur within democratic dyads. This "empty-margin" problem renders inapplicable latent-variable models (e.g., logit or probit) and Poisson models.[27] An alternative, the linear probability model, is problematic if applied to very rare events.

As a result, two approaches are taken here to examine the relationship between polity type and the probability of war. First, Pearson χ^2 statistics

[26] Complete results can be obtained from the authors. See chap. 6, n.5, for the exception.
[27] Both yield unbounded estimates where there is an empty margin. Bremer (1992b; 1993) applies a Poisson model to the analysis of democracy and conflict, avoiding the empty-margin problem by aggregating across time periods.

are computed from two-way breakdowns of polity type by war, and these are used to test the hypothesis of independence of polity type and conflict.[28] A strength of this approach is that it is straightforward and robust to underlying distributional assumptions. A weakness of the bivariate approach is that there may be important omitted variables that could bias the estimated relationship between polity type and the probability of war.[29]

Thus, a second approach is used to test the hypothesis that no relationship exists between polity type and the probability of war. The test has two stages. In the first stage, the null hypothesis that polity types and war rates are independent is maintained. A probit model of the probability of war is estimated as a function of a set of control variables (i.e., contiguity and major-power status) that does not include polity type, using the sample of all relevant dyad-years. In the second stage, these estimates and the sample of democratic dyads are used to predict the probability of occurrence of no more than the number of wars actually observed between members of democratic dyads.

If this predicted probability is larger than some critical level (e.g., 0.05), the null hypothesis that polity types and war rates are independent (i.e., the same process produces all wars) is not rejected. If, however, this probability is smaller than the critical level, the null hypothesis is rejected in favor of the alternative that democratic dyads are less war prone.[30]

THE RESULTS

The Aggregate Analysis

In order to verify that the data yield results consistent with those of previous studies, the entire 1816–1980 period, including the periods of the

[28] Caution is required in testing hypotheses regarding such rare events as war. However, the Pearson χ^2 statistic is generally recognized to be appropriate as long as the expected cell sizes under the null hypothesis of independence are all greater than one (Fienberg 1980, 170). In the analyses in this chapter the minimum expected cell size (the expected number of wars between democracies) is always substantially larger than one, so that the conditions for appropriate use of the Pearson χ^2 statistic are met throughout.

[29] This same problem applies to models that compare, e.g., the probability of conflict between allied and nonallied democracies or nondemocracies (Maoz 1997, 176–78).

[30] Spiro (1994) uses a similar method, although he uses a very restrictive definition of liberal dyads in his multiyear analyses. (For further discussion of Spiro's analysis, see Russett [1995].) Note that a test procedure analogous to that outlined here can be used to test the null hypothesis of no relationship between regime type and the probability of war against the alternative that democratic dyads are more war-prone than nondemocratic dyads.

TABLE 4.1
Probability of War and Lower-Level MIDs by Polity Type, 1816–1980:
Fraction of Dyad-Years in Conflict

| | Polity type | | | |
	Democratic-democratic	Other	χ^2 statistic	p-value
Wars	0.0002 [30963]	0.0011 [275807]	20.35	0.000
Lower-level MIDs	0.0029 [27662]	0.0048 [244098]	18.52	0.000

Note: The χ^2 statistics are the Pearson statistics for tests of independence of the polity type and the probability of war and lower-level disputes for each period. The numbers in brackets are sample sizes.

two world wars and the interwar years, is examined first. Of the 306,770 dyad-years in this analysis, 304 are dyad-years of war. Seven of these involve democratic dyads: one of these is the Spanish-American War; the six others pair Finland with various allied nations and the United States in World War II (Small and Singer 1982).[31]

The results of this preliminary analysis conform to those of other studies. Table 4.1 presents the results of a bivariate analysis of wars and disputes between democracies. It shows that both wars and lower-level disputes occur at a significantly lower rate than do wars between members of other pairs of states across the entire 1816–1980 time period. The probability of war between democracies is 0.02 percent, while that of all other dyads is 0.11 percent. The corresponding statistics for disputes short of war are 0.29 and 0.48. Pearson χ^2 tests of independence of polity type and the probability of war or other disputes clearly rejects independence (p-value < 0.0005 for both).[32]

Table 4.2 presents the results of a multivariate probit analysis of war and lower-level disputes across the 1816–1980 period, controlling for the number of major powers in a dyad and for contiguity. These results

[31] To reiterate, this is the only analysis which includes the Finnish dyads, as the World War II years are subsequently dropped from the analyses.

[32] During World War I, no difference in lower-level MID rates by regime type exists (p-value = 0.146). During the Second World War, members of democratic dyads are significantly less likely to engage each other in lower-level MIDs than are members of other dyads (p-value = 0.019).

TABLE 4.2
Probit Analysis of Probability of War and Lower-Level MIDs,
1816–1980

Variables	Wars	Lower-level MIDs
Constant	−0.0061**	−0.0190**
	(0.0005)	(0.0006)
Democratic	−0.0010**	0.0020**
	(0.0002)	(0.0003)
Contiguous	0.0010**	0.0060**
	(0.0001)	(0.0002)
1 Major power	0.0009**	0.0029**
	(0.0001)	(0.0002)
2 Major powers	0.0016**	0.0055**
	(0.0002)	(0.0004)
Log L	−2135.5	−6495.9
Sample size	306770	271760

Note: The numbers in parentheses are standard errors, corrected for arbitrary heteroscedacity using Huber's formula. The coefficients are normalized to represent the derivative of the probability of the outcome with respect to a change in the explanatory variable. This is computed as $\beta\phi(\overline{X}\beta)$ where β is the vector of estimated parameters of the probit model, $\overline{X}$ is the vector of means of the explanatory variables, and ϕ is the standard normal probability density function. The sample mean war rate is 0.0010; the sample mean rate for other disputes is 0.0046. *p-value < 0.05, two-tailed test. **p-value < 0.01, two-tailed test.

are also consistent with the earlier studies. As table 4.2 shows, members of pairs of democratic states are significantly less likely to engage each other in war and other militarized disputes than are members of other country pairs (p-value < 0.0005). The effects of major powers and contiguity are positive and statistically significant (all at p-values < 0.0005).

Disaggregating the Data

Next examined is whether war probabilities differ across the pre-1914, interwar, and post-1945 periods. Because the periods of the world wars

TABLE 4.3

Probability of War by Polity Type and Time-Period: Fraction of Dyad-Years at War

| Time period | Polity type | | χ^2 statistic | p-value |
	Democratic-democratic	Other		
Pre–World War I (1816–1913)	0.0007 [1475]	0.0015 [53915]	0.660	0.417
Interwar (1919–38)	0.0000 [5919]	0.0003 [31483]	1.881	0.170
Post–World War II (1946–80)	0.0000 [22498]	0.0004 [176203]	8.174	0.004

Note: The χ^2 statistics are the Pearson statistics for tests of independence of the polity type and the probability of war for each period. The numbers in brackets are sample sizes.

are dropped, there is only one war between democracies in the sample (the Spanish-American War). Interstate war of any kind, however, is a rare event. Thus, the question focused upon is whether a statistically significant and consistent difference exists between the war rates of democratic and other dyads.

Table 4.3 contains the probability of war by polity type for each period. The table also contains Pearson χ^2 statistics for tests of independence of polity type and the probability of war. These results show that a consistently significant relationship between polity type and the probability of war does not exist across the time periods.

More specifically, no significant relationship exists between polity type and the probability of war before 1914 (p-value = 0.417).[33] This result does not depend on whether or not the Spanish-American War is included.[34] Nor does dyadic regime type affect the probability of war between 1919 and 1939 (p-value = 0.170).[35] After World War II, however,

[33] The finding of no statistically significant difference cannot be interpreted as simply a function of the relatively small size of the pre-1914 sample: no statistically significant difference between democratic and other dyads would exist even if the sample size was inflated by a factor of 10. More evidence on this point is contained in chapter 7.

[34] The p-value of the χ^2 statistic testing independence of regime type and the probability of war is 0.21 if Spain is reclassified as a nondemocracy.

[35] According to Maoz, a reanalysis based on a more complete version of the MID data

TABLE 4.4
Probit Analysis of Probability of War

Variable	Pre-1914	1919–1938	Post-1945
Constant	−0.0105	−0.0027**	−0.0026**
	(0.0012)	(0.0009)	(0.0004)
Contiguous	0.0019**		0.0006**
	(0.0003)		(0.0001)
1 Major power	0.0006*	0.0003**	0.0002**
	(0.0003)	(0.0001)	(0.0001)
2 Major powers	0.0006	0.0006**	0.0005**
	(0.0005)	(0.0003)	(0.0002)
Log L	−570.8	−88.3	−519.0
Sample size	55390	37402	198701

Note: The numbers in parentheses are standard errors, corrected for arbitrary heteroscedacity using Huber's formula. The coefficients are normalized to represent the derivative of the probability of the outcome with respect to a change in the explanatory variable. This is computed as $\beta\phi(\overline{X}\beta)$ where β is the vector of estimated parameters of the probit model, $\overline{X}$ is the vector of means of the explanatory variables, and ϕ is the standard normal probability density function. The sample mean war rates for each period respectively are 0.0015, 0.0031, and 0.0003. *p-value < 0.05, two-tailed test. **p-value < 0.01, two-tailed test.

members of democratic dyads are significantly less likely to fight each other than are members of other dyads (p-value $= 0.004$).

The estimates of the probit model used as the basis of the two-stage test described above are presented in table 4.4, which contains estimates of probit models of the probability of war as a function of contiguity and major-power status, based on the null hypothesis that polity type and war

does not support the pre–World War II findings here or those reported earlier (Farber and Gowa 1995). More precisely, he says, "Farber and Gowa's findings on the higher war rates . . . [of democratic dyads] in the pre-1946 periods were not replicated by the present analysis" (1997, 167) However, it should be clear that the results reported here and earlier (Farber and Gowa 1995; 1997) show only that there was no statistically significant difference between relative dyadic war rates before 1914 or between the wars. Thus, the only difference between Maoz's war results and those here is his finding that nondemocracies have a significantly higher war rate than do democracies between 1919 and 1938 (1997, 168).

rates are independent. These estimates show that the probability of war is significantly related to contiguity both before World War I and after World War II (p-value < 0.0005).[36] The number of major powers in a dyad also has a statistically significant effect on the probability of war in all three periods (p-value <0.03).

Next is a test of the null hypothesis. One war involving a democratic dyad occurs prior to World War I. Using the estimates in the first column of table 4.4, the probability that there is one or fewer wars for the 1,475 democratic dyad-years is 0.141. Thus, for the pre-1914 period, the null hypothesis that the same process that produces wars in general also produces wars between democracies cannot be rejected.

There are no wars between democratic dyads during the interwar years. Using the estimates in the second column of table 4.2, the probability of no wars for the 5,919 democratic dyad-years in this period is 0.158. Again, it is not possible to reject the null hypothesis.

No wars occur between democratic states in the post–World War II period. The estimates in the third column of table 4.4 predict that there is a 0.00001 probability of no wars for the 22,498 democratic dyad-years in this period. For the Cold War years, then, the hypothesis that the process that generates wars in general also generates war between democracies can clearly be rejected.

The results of the multivariate analyses are clear: there is no consistent evidence of a significant relationship between polity type and the incidence of war across the pre–World War I and the post–World War II international systems. What has become conventional wisdom about the effect of democracies on war applies only to the Cold War years.

MIDs

Next, the relative incidence of lower-level disputes across time is analyzed. Table 4.5 contains the probability of lower-level MIDs by polity type for each time period. The table also contains Pearson χ^2 statistics for tests of independence of polity type and the probability of lower-level MIDs. Again, the table shows that there is no consistent relationship between polity type and dispute probabilities.

Of particular interest are the results for the pre-World War I period. The table shows that the probability of MIDs short of war is significantly

---

[36] There are no wars between members of noncontiguous dyads in the interwar period. This creates an empty-margin problem, and, as a result, the model for the interwar period does not control for contiguity.

TABLE 4.5

Probability of Lower-Level MIDs by Polity Type and Time-Period: Fraction of Dyad-Years in Lower-Level MIDs

	Polity type			
Time period	Democratic-democratic	Other	χ^2 statistic	p-value
Pre–World War I (1817–1913)	0.0177 [1470]	0.0075 [53502]	19.40	<0.0005
Interwar (1919–38)	0.0032 [5913]	0.0037 [31403]	0.2801	0.5970
Post–World War II (1946–76)	0.0017 [19198]	0.0032 [145145]	13.75	<0.0005

Note: The χ^2 statistics are the Pearson statistics for tests of independence of the polity type and the probability of lower-level disputes for each period. The numbers in brackets are sample sizes.

higher for members of democratic dyads than for members of other dyad types prior to World War I (p-value < 0.0005).[37] No statistically significant difference exists between the wars (p-value = 0.597). However, during the Cold War, members of democratic dyads engage each other in these disputes at a significantly lower rate than do members of other dyads (p-value < 0.0005).

Table 4.6 contains probit analyses of the probability of lower-level MIDs that control for polity type, contiguity, and major-power status. In all three periods, the presence of one or more major powers in a dyad, as well as contiguity, are statistically significant (p-value < 0.0005).

For the pre-1914 period, the multivariate analysis yields somewhat different results than does the bivariate analysis. Table 4.6 shows that the lower-level dispute rate of members of democratic dyads does not differ from that of members of other country pairs before World War I (p-value = 0.161). Between the wars, disputes between democracies occur at a significantly lower rate than do those between other states (p-value = 0.005). The same is true after World War II (p-value < 0.0005).[38]

[37] In part, this reflects the fact that the U.K. and the U.S. are the two most dispute-prone nations in the MID data set (Gochman and Maoz 1984, 609). The U.K. is coded as a democracy as of 1837; the U.S. is so coded throughout.

[38] Maoz and Russett (1993) established the post-1945 result earlier.

65

TABLE 4.6
Probit Analysis of Probability of Lower-Level MIDs

Variable	Pre-1914	1919–38	Post-1945
Constant	0.0362**	− 0.0085**	0.0128**
	(0.0018)	(0.0012)	(0.0008)
Democratic	0.0016	− 0.0007**	− 0.0019**
	(0.0011)	(0.0003)	(0.0003)
Contiguous	0.0095**	0.0030**	0.0051**
	(0.0006)	(0.0004)	(0.0003)
1 Major power	0.0038**	0.0013**	0.0015**
	(0.0006)	(0.0003)	(0.0002)
2 Major powers	0.0080**	0.0031**	0.0050**
	(0.0011)	(0.0006)	(0.0006)
Log L	− 2181.8	− 633.9	− 2694.7
Sample size	54972	37316	164343

Note: The numbers in parentheses are standard errors, corrected for arbitrary hetero-scedacity using Huber's formula. The coefficients are normalized to represent the derivative of the probability of the outcome with respect to a change in the explanatory variable. This is computed as $\beta\phi(\overline{X}\beta)$ where β is the vector of estimated parameters of the probit model, $\overline{X}$ is the vector of means of the explanatory variables, and ϕ is the standard normal probability density function. The sample mean dispute rate is 0.0078 before 1914, 0.0036 between the wars, and 0.0031 after 1945. *p-value < 0.05, two-tailed test. **p-value < 0.01, two-tailed test.

It is interesting to note the relative magnitude of the joint-democracy effect, that is, its impact rather than its statistical significance. Table 4.6 shows that members of democratic dyads are 0.19 percentage points less likely to engage in a militarized dispute than are the members of other country pairs after 1945, relative to the mean dispute rate of 0.31 percentage points for the sample as a whole. In comparison, if the members of a dyad are contiguous or are both major powers, the probability of a dispute between them increases by 0.51 percentage points.

CONCLUSION

The analyses in this chapter shows that violent disputes do not occur at a consistently lower rate between democracies than between other states.

More specifically, they show that the war and lower-level MID rates of democratic and nondemocratic dyads do not differ significantly before 1914. Between 1919 and 1938, democracies are no less likely than are other states to engage each other in wars, although they are less likely to become involved in lower-level disputes. After 1945, democratic states are less likely than are their nondemocratic counterparts to engage each other in either war or MIDs short of war.

The democratic-peace hypothesis predicts that the war and lower-level dispute rates of democratic dyads should be uniformly lower than are those of their nondemocratic counterparts. Thus, the finding that relative dyadic dispute rates vary across time is inconsistent with it. In the next chapter, I begin to examine an alternative explanation, based on common and conflicting interests, of this cross-temporal variation in dispute-rate patterns.

Interests and Alliances:
Comparing Two International Systems

THE RESULTS presented in the last chapter do not conform to the predictions of the democratic-peace hypothesis. However, they are consistent with conventional wisdom about major-power interactions in the pre-1914 multipolar international system and in its post–World War II bipolar replacement. That is, the interests of major powers, irrespective of regime type, were relatively fluid before World War I. After 1945, however, an enduring conflict of interests between the superpowers generated a pattern of consistent common interests between democratic states.

Cross-temporal variation in relative dyadic dispute-rate patterns seems to reflect this difference. All else equal, states that have interests in common are less likely to engage each other in militarized disputes than are those with interests in conflict. Thus, the heterogeneity that characterizes major-power interactions before 1914 is consistent with the finding that relative dyadic dispute rates do not differ as a function of polity type before World War I. Analogously, that common interests existed between democratic states during the Cold War is consistent with the finding that democratic dyads have a lower dispute rate than do other dyads after 1945.

In this chapter I examine whether interest patterns do, in fact, vary across international systems as conventional wisdom assumes. First, I discuss briefly the concept of state interests, and I explain the use of alliances as a proxy for them. Then I briefly review the evolution of major-power interests and alliances between 1870 and 1903 and between 1946 and 1961. I conclude that alliances seem to be a reasonable substitute for a more direct measure of interests. I also conclude that conventional wisdom does seem to capture important changes in interest patterns between pairs of democratic states and other country pairs across the centuries.

INTERESTS AND ALLIANCES

In the democratic-peace literature, as in the second-image literature more generally, domestic politics shape the preferences of states. In the third-image or realist literature, however, domestic politics and preferences are independent of each other: it is the logic of situations that determines state interests.[1] Among the most important situational influences are the anarchic structure of the international system and the existence of asymmetric information (Jervis 1978; Kydd 1997; Waltz 1979).

In the realist view, an impending or actual shift in the balance of power generates common interests among those states that it threatens. Realist theory expects each of those placed at risk to engage in "balancing" behavior, that is, to increase its power in response, either by reallocating domestic resources between guns and butter or by forming alliances with other threatened states.[2] It does not expect balancing behavior to vary as a function of regime type.

That situations such as a changing distribution of power can define state interests is not hard to grasp. Nor is it difficult to understand that national survival is the interest at stake when the power distribution is fluid. Nonetheless, interests can be difficult to measure even under this condition. This is so, in part, because relative changes in material power are not always clear, nor is the motivation for them observable.[3] The same is true of resolve, a crucial indicator of state interests in given situations: it cannot be communicated directly; instead, it must be inferred from state behavior.[4] Deducing interests can also be difficult, because states that prefer to free ride on the deterrent efforts of others have incentives to obscure rather than to reveal their interests.

In important domains of international relations, then, state preferences are not directly observable and, as a result, are very difficult to measure. Students of international relations, therefore, often use the presence or absence of political-military alliances as a proxy for interests (e.g., Bueno de Mesquita 1981; Bueno de Mesquita and Lalman 1992; Dixon 1994; Siverson and Emmons 1991; Siverson and Starr 1991).[5] This solution

---

[1] As Waltz puts it, "internationally, different states have produced similar as well as different outcomes, and similar states have produced different as well as similar outcomes" (1979, 37).

[2] For analyses that suggest that states will sometimes "bandwagon" rather than balance, see, e.g., Christensen and Snyder (1990); Schweller (1994).

[3] This, of course, creates grave problems for states contemplating the adoption of a strategy of appeasement (see, e.g., Powell 1996b) and is a principal cause of war (e.g., Fearon 1994).

[4] For discussion, see Walt (1987, 12).

[5] Gartzke (1998) uses an index of "national affinity," based on the cross-national correlation of roll-call votes in the United Nations between 1950 and 1985, to construct a measure of common interests.

creates a problem of its own, however: by definition, alliances imperfectly measure the existence of common interests.

This measurement error has several sources. Sometimes, the strength of common interests between countries can be so clear that a formal alliance has no value added (e.g., the United States and Israel after 1948); a tacit alliance, however, leaves no trace in the data. At other times, the conversion of a tacit treaty to a formal alliance can reflect increasing tensions rather a strengthening of common interests (e.g., the Soviet-Egyptian Treaty of Friendship and Alliance). Formal alliances can also endure long after they have evolved into "paper tigers" (e.g., the Sino-Soviet alliance).

Alliances may also be the product of induced "common" interests (Schroeder 1976). The Warsaw Treaty Organization (WTO) is a good case in point. The creation of an alliance like the WTO obviously requires some power asymmetry among its members. Why the formalization of ties enhances the ability of the dominant state to control its "allies" is unclear, however. If it does so because the allies receive side payments, the alliance terms of trade will be more skewed in their favor than conventional analyses suggest. Some, albeit minimal, common interests, then, seem to exist even in cases of induced alliances.

Historical Patterns

In this section, I examine more systematically the extent to which alliances are a good proxy for the underlying theoretical variable of interests. To do so, I analyze interactions among members of the major-power subsystem. I limit the analysis to major powers for two reasons. First, these states dominate the creation and maintenance of international systems. Second, an exclusive focus on the major powers keeps the historical analysis tractable.

Analytic tractability also motivates the relatively brief time periods I examine. I trace the evolution of major-power interests and alliances between 1871 and 1903 and between 1946 and 1961. A review of these periods should yield insights into whether important differences exist between the pre–World War I and post–World War II systems, although obviously not to the same extent as more comprehensive historical analyses of these periods (see, e.g., Albrecht-Carrié 1973; Bradley 1989; Campbell 1962; Cronin 1996; Gilbert 1991; Hogan 1987; Kennedy 1980; Langer 1931; Milward 1984; Wesseling 1996).

Because these analyses are based on a nonrandom selection of years and states, they are necessarily suggestive rather than conclusive. However, a historical analysis of the interest and alliance patterns of all states during all years is beyond the scope of this study. As in small-n studies more generally, the value of these analyses inheres in their ability to cast light on the causal patterns that theoretical studies suggest exist.[6]

Major Powers, Interests, and Alliances: 1871–1903

THE SAMPLE

According to Small and Singer (1982, 45), England, France, Austria-Hungary, Italy, and Russia are major powers during the entire 1871–1903 period. (Germany replaces Prussia in 1871.) Japan achieves major-power status in 1895, at the end of the Sino-Japanese War. The United States become a major power as of the conclusion of the Spanish-American War in 1898. Appendix 5.A lists the major-power alliances that the COW project records between 1871 and 1903, as well as their duration.

OVERVIEW

Some major-power conflicts of interests persist throughout this period. For example, Germany and France never resolve the conflicts that the Franco-Prussian War engendered, and Austria-Hungary and Russia engage in a continuing competition for spheres of influence in the Balkans. Britain and France come to near blows over Egypt, while Britain and Russia remain perpetually at odds over Asia and the Near East.

Other interest patterns are much more fluid, however. Britain and Italy sometimes render support to Austria-Hungary. Germany does so more consistently, although typically with some wariness born of its concern about alienating Russia. Britain sometimes seeks German assistance, as do France and Russia. Germany, Britain, and Austria-Hungary cooperate against Russia in the Balkans, while Germany, Britain, and Russia cooperate with each other against Japan in Asia.

HISTORICAL NARRATIVE

This period begins with the emergence of a new continental balance-of-power system. In the wake of the Franco-Prussian War, Germany becomes the preeminent power on the European continent. For most of

---

[6] For a very clear and useful discussion of the utility of small-n analyses, see Ray (1995, chap. 4).

the period examined here, maintaining European stability is Germany's primary goal. In an effort to attain it, Berlin adopts a strategy designed to isolate France and to sustain good relations with, as well as between, Austria-Hungary and Russia.

Successful pursuit of this strategy would eventually founder in the Balkans. As the Ottoman Empire disintegrated, the great powers disagreed about how to manage the process. A rapid dismantling would serve German interests in European stability and Russian interests in the Turkish Straits, because it would permit a division of the Balkans into spheres of influence. For the same reason, however, it would place at risk British interests in the Mediterranean, as well as the territorial integrity of the Austro-Hungarian Empire.

In an attempt to contain the potential for major-power conflict in the Balkans, Bismarck, the German Imperial Chancellor, established the "Three Emperors League" in 1873. Serendipity helped to create the *Dreikaiserbund*: at the time, domestic issues preoccupied Russia, and Austria-Hungary preferred to defer conflict in the Balkans until its relative power increased. Nonetheless, given the conflicting interests of St. Petersburg and Vienna, the *Dreikaiserbund* rested on fragile foundations that would crumble as tensions in the area escalated.

In 1876, after a series of revolts in the Balkans, Serbia and Montenegro waged an unsuccessful war against Turkey. In its aftermath, concerns about the regional power balance intensified in Russia. In exchange for its promise to refrain from creating a large Balkan state, Russia secured a pledge of neutrality from Vienna and declared war on Turkey in 1877. The Treaty of San Stefano that ended the Russian-Turkish War allowed for the creation of a Greater Bulgaria, affording Russia access to the Aegean Sea at the expense of violating its prewar pledge to Austria. Serbia, Montenegro, and Rumania were granted independence, and Russia gained additional territory in the region (Lowe 1994, 49).

Russian gains would prove short-lived, however. Austria-Hungary objected to the prospective shift in the balance of power, and the threat of Russian control over the Straits precipitated British preparations for war. As a result, the Congress of Berlin deprived Russia of its most important war spoils: it lost access to the Aegean, as Eastern Roumelia, Macedonia, and Bulgaria replaced what would have been Greater Bulgaria.

The great-power dynamics evident at the Congress, as well as the conclusion of a defense pact between Berlin and Vienna in 1879, intensified tensions between Russia and Austria-Hungary and decreased Russian confidence in German support. Nonetheless, two years later, the three powers renewed the *Dreikaiserbund*. As before, isolating France and containing Russian expansion in the Balkans motivated Germany, while Russia sought to preclude an Anglo-Austrian alliance and to constrain Vienna in the Balkans. Vienna acquiesced because it had no other choice: its British option had expired when the Tories assumed office in 1880.[7]

However, the *Dreikaiserbund* would not survive another Balkan crisis. The Bulgarian crisis created an acute conflict of interests between Austria-Hungary and Russia, leading Russia to denounce the Three Emperors League. Vienna turned to Germany for support. Because Berlin had pledged to support Russian ambitions in the Near East, however, Vienna found a more willing ally in Britain. Prompted by their common interest in containing Russian power, Austria-Hungary, Britain, and Italy signed the first and second Mediterranean Agreements in February and December 1887, respectively.

The conclusion of the Reinsurance Treaty between Germany and Russia in June of the same year reflects a somewhat different constellation of interests. Germany wanted to preempt a Franco-Russian alliance and restore stability to the Balkans, while Russia wanted Germany to remain neutral in the event Austria-Hungary attacked it. Thus, the treaty insured St. Petersburg against German intervention in the event of an Austrian attack and Berlin against Russian intervention in case of a Franco-German war.

Three years later, however, the increasing power of Germany and political shifts within it led Berlin to refuse to renew the accord. As a result, France and Russia signed an entente in 1891 and a military convention three years later. Their decision to do so reflected both their common enmity toward Germany and the fact that neither had recourse to any potential great-power ally except the other. Long-standing conflicts between Russia and Britain in Asia precluded any Anglo-Russian agreement, while Anglo-French conflicts gave Paris no alternative to Russia.

In the Anglo-French case, control over Egypt provoked probably the most severe conflict of interests between the two powers. The construction of the Suez Canal in 1869 gave Britain a strong interest in controlling Egypt, nominally part of the Ottoman Empire. Its opportunity to do so arose in 1878, when Egyptian inability to service its debts led to the creation of an International Commission on the Public Debt with six

[7] To placate Vienna, Bismarck signed the Triple Alliance in 1882. Because the treaty pledged Italy to remain neutral in the event of a war between Vienna and St. Petersburg, it allowed Austria-Hungary to redeploy several troop divisions to Vienna's eastern frontier (Taylor 1962, 555).

members: two each from Britain and France and one each from Austria and Italy. The appointment of British and French ministers to the Egyptian cabinet allowed London and Paris to gain dual control over Egypt.

Four years later, in the wake of a military revolt against the Egyptian government, both countries deployed warships to the eastern Mediterranean. A British sea and land assault enabled London to gain unilateral control over Egypt, thereby imposing on France what has been described as its "worst humiliation since Sedan" (Robinson 1962, 602). The ensuing tensions between London and Paris would persist for almost two decades.

Indeed, in 1898, the Fashoda crisis would bring London and Paris to the brink of war. Britain had earlier dispatched forces to the area under General Horatio Kitchener to regain control of the Sudan. In the interim, however, the French had begun to try to regain influence in Egypt by constructing a dam to control the flow of the Nile River at Fashoda, some four hundred miles south of Khartoum. In September 1898, General Kitchener's forces met those of French Captain Jean-Baptise Marchand.[8]

Until November, it was "touch and go [about] whether France and Britain would fight each other—not simply for Fashoda but for what that lonely place symbolized: to the British, safety in Egypt and in India; to the French, security in the Mediterranean" (Robinson 1962, 629). Recognizing its relatively weak position in the region and the more general threat to its security that an Anglo-French conflict would provoke, France backed down. In the process, France and Russia agreed to mobilize forces in the event Britain attacked either (Snyder 1997, 106).

In addition to the conflict between Britain and France with respect to Egypt, a serious Anglo-French crisis developed in Asia. In 1892–93, France advanced into Siam from Indochina, while Russia advanced into Afghanistan. Relations between London and Paris became so tense that it seemed to some that the next great war would pit Britain against either or both Russia and France, "with Germany and Austria (at least in the opening phases) in the role of interested by-standers" (Bartlett 1996, 121).

In the late nineteenth century, major-power conflict and cooperation also extended to China, precipitating another interest alignment. Its loss in the 1895 Sino-Japanese War forced China to accept a puppet state in Korea and to cede the Liaotung Peninsula, including Port Arthur. For

---

[8] This paragraph is based on Ray (1995, 176–77).

different reasons, Russia, France, and Germany, however, preferred the status quo ex ante: Russia sought control over areas on the mainland that Japan had forced China to cede; France and Germany agreed to avoid alienating Russia; and Britain abstained (Snyder 1997, 103).

This settlement was short-lived, however. In November 1897, Germany occupied the Chinese port of Kiao-Chow. In response, Russia occupied Port Arthur in December. Shortly thereafter, Russia demanded that China lease the Liaotung Peninsula to it to enable the construction of a link between Port Arthur and the Trans-Siberian Railroad, and it secured a loan from France to facilitate the construction. During the Boxer Rebellion, Russia effectively occupied Manchuria (Lowe 1994, 113–15).

In an effort to gain support for its interests in Manchuria and in China more generally, Britain turned to Germany. The two countries had little in common, however: Britain sought German help to contain Russian influence in China, while Germany wanted British help to contain Russia in Europe. Because Russian interests in China and Korea conflicted with those of Japan, Tokyo proved more receptive to British overtures (Lowe 1994, 116). As a result, the two countries signed the Anglo-Japanese Treaty in 1902.

This agreement responded to concerns about the regional power balance in Asia. More generally, however, it signaled increasing British concerns about the balance of power in Europe. Berlin had begun to construct its high seas fleet. Admiral von Tirpitz, chief of the naval staff, believed that the fleet's construction would force Britain to come to terms with German power. Tirpitz miscalculated, however.

London chose a very different strategy. It allied with Japan, partly because doing so allowed it to redeploy some of its naval forces from the Far East to the North Sea (Lowe 1994, 155). The German naval buildup also led Britain to an effort to settle its conflicts with France (Langhorne 1981, 45).[9] An Anglo-French detente would allow Britain to redeploy its naval forces from the Eastern Mediterranean to the North Sea, as well as increase the probability of an Anglo-Russian accord.

An opportunity to reach an understanding with France arose when the latter sought to control Morocco to protect its interests in Algeria. The price of German acquiescence was French renunciation of Alsace and

---

[9] Domestic politics also played an important role in the construction of the German navy, as industrial interests supported its buildup. The Prussians were the natural constituents of the German land forces.

Lorraine (White 1995, 26). Britain's terms were far less onerous: French cession of its claims in Egypt, already tenuous because of the secular decline in French leverage as Egyptian debts fell (Fay 1928, 167).

The weak domestic regime in Russia and the danger of a Russo-Japanese war also facilitated the signing of an Anglo-French accord. Because Russia was allied to France and Britain was allied to Japan, a war between St. Petersburg and Tokyo threatened to embroil Britain and France in a war against each other. Not a desirable prospect at any time, it seemed suicidal as the German threat steadily increased. Thus, London and Paris signed what became known as the Entente Cordiale early in 1904.[10]

Its conclusion marked the beginning of a very different pattern of major-power interactions: the division of the great powers into pro- and anti-German coalitions. As the German threat crystallized, the issues that had divided France, Britain, Russia, and Japan from each other faded into insignificance. The 1905 Moroccan Crisis strengthened the Anglo-French entente and contributed to the conclusion of the Anglo-Russian entente two years later. Between 1904 and the outbreak of World War I, alliance blocs became progressively "bipolarized," marking a fundamental change in major-power relations from the pattern that had prevailed for thirty years after the Franco-Prussian War.

Major Powers, Interests, and Alliances: 1946–1961

THE SAMPLE

I begin this narrative in the first year of the postwar world and conclude it with the dissolution of the Sino-Soviet alliance. The set of major powers in this period includes the United States, the Soviet Union, France, Britain, and China (Small and Singer 1982).[11] Appendix 5.B lists the alliances these states concluded between themselves during the sample period, as well as their duration.

[10] Three years earlier, the German naval threat had also motivated Britain to settle its episodic disputes with the United States. The issue that precipitated the settlement was the Panama Canal. Demanding exclusive control of the canal, the United States sought to deprive Britain of the rights it had gained in the Clayton-Bulwer Treaty of 1850. In the 1901 Hay-Pauncefote Treaty, the British essentially conceded their rights over the canal to the United States. They did so, in part, in order to facilitate a redeployment of their ships from the Western Hemisphere to their home waters.

[11] Based on the extent to which scholarly consensus exists about membership in the post-1945 major-power set, Small and Singer consider their assignment of major-power status to the United States, the Soviet Union, and Britain as unproblematic. They consider their assignment of similar status to France and China as "reasonable" (1982, 45).

I focus here on three issues central to an understanding of the evolution of state preferences in the immediate postwar period: the disintegration of the common interests that bound Britain, the Soviet Union, and the United States together during World War II; the emergence of strong ties between the United States, Britain, and France; and the origins of the Sino-Soviet split.

THE WARTIME ALLIANCE

To explain the breakdown of the wartime alliance between the United States, Britain, and the Soviet Union, it helps to recall Winston Churchill's comment on the eve of the German invasion of the U.S.S.R.: "If Hitler invaded Hell I would make at least a favourable reference to the Devil in the House of Commons" (cited in Waltz 1979, 166). Winning the war had superseded the conflicts of interests that had earlier divided Britain and the U.S.S.R., as well as the United States and the Soviet Union; its end allowed old conflicts to reemerge and new conflicts to surface.

Among them, the most corrosive would, of course, involve the reconstruction of Europe. Although a Soviet fait accompli established what would become the postwar status quo in Eastern Europe, the issue of Germany remained to be resolved. At Yalta the Big Three agreed to levy reparations on Germany on the order of $20 billion, of which the U.S.S.R. was to receive half. Initially, the Morgenthau Plan and Soviet ideas about the role of Germany in the postwar system also coincided: Germany would be rendered politically impotent; its economy was to be dominated by agriculture.

Soon after the conclusion of the Yalta Conference, however, the United States adopted the British plan of rehabilitating Germany. To achieve their goal, the two countries suspended German reparations flows and merged their occupation zones in January 1947. Negotiations to find a four-power solution to the German question at the London Conference of Foreign Ministers failed, and the Soviets left the Allied Control Council in March 1948. Shortly thereafter, Britain, the United States, and France agreed to implement currency reforms in Germany and liberalize its economy, precipitating the Berlin blockade of 1948–49 (Dunbabin 1994, 86–96).

The conflict over the reconstruction of Europe, as well as a series of disputes over other issues, ensured that almost nothing remained of the wartime alliance as of mid-1948. The end of the Second World War had eliminated its raison d'être. An irreconcilable conflict of interests about the balance of power in Europe supplanted it. The East-West split would endure until the Soviet Union collapsed in 1989.

THE CONVERGENCE OF WESTERN INTERESTS

A common theme of the early postwar literature is that U.S. power allowed the United States to reconstruct Western Europe in its own image. Thus, it was not an accident that both the French and Italian governing coalitions expelled the Communist Party, nor was it mere coincidence that U.S. interests and the shape of the postwar economic and security order coincided. Indeed, the NATO alliance, this literature suggests, conforms more closely to a coalition created to manage its members than to a reflection of the common interests among them.[12]

Archival evidence that became available only after the first wave of Cold War literature appeared, however, suggests that a series of transatlantic bargains, rather than the unilateral imposition of U.S. interests, led to NATO's formation.[13] As the brief review here suggests, British and, to a lesser extent, French power remained sufficient to ensure that NATO did not reflect U.S. preferences alone. Thus, common interests lay at the core of the major postwar alliance among the democratic countries.

The conclusion of the Dunkirk Treaty in 1947 marked an important first step toward NATO's creation. In the immediate aftermath of World War II, Britain and France shared an intense concern about German power—that is, "a sense of a mutual, newly confirmed nearness in the face of danger"—that a geographically remote United States lacked. They also shared a belief in the importance of military power, while the United States "remained stubbornly attached to the belief that everything could be solved through economic aid" (Barié 1991, 44–5). Their concerns about Germany led Britain and France to conclude the Treaty of Dunkirk on March 14, 1947.[14]

Shortly after the London Conference of Foreign Ministers ended, British Foreign Secretary Ernest Bevin, in a now famous speech to the House

[12] As noted earlier, an example of this type of alliance is the WTO, which the U.S.S.R. established in 1955 to secure its western border, among other interests (e.g., legalizing the presence of Soviet troops in Hungary and Romania) (Lewis 1994, 191).

[13] Benjamin J. Cohen first described the postwar Bretton Woods monetary system as the product of a "transatlantic bargain" (1974). Risse-Kappen (1995) contends that the same bargaining characterizes important cases of U.S. foreign policy during the Cold War.

[14] The treaty, however, lacked any formidable deterrent power. It involved no provisions for joint military planning. Britain believed that military cooperation with France would compromise its security, given communist control of the French Ministry of Defense during early 1947 (De Leonardis 1991, 185).

of Commons, proposed the creation of a Western Union. His initiative responded in part to the U.S. refusal to commit itself to defend Europe until the Europeans themselves had made a tangible commitment to their collective self-defense.

Britain and France intended originally to construct a series of bilateral agreements between themselves and each of the Benelux countries. Pressure from the Benelux countries and the United States, as well as the 1948 Czech coup, however, persuaded Britain and France to agree to a multilateral expansion of the Treaty of Dunkirk (Crockatt 1995, 79). The Brussels Treaty, therefore, marked an important advance toward a transatlantic, multilateral alliance. Signed on March 17, 1948, it established the Western European Union, which committed its signatories to render military assistance to each other in the event of aggression against their metropolitarian territories (Wiebes and Zeeman 1991, 154).[15]

As the Brussels Treaty was signed, Secretary of State George Marshall invited Britain and Canada to begin talks about a transatlantic alliance (Smith 1991, 64).[16] Further progress, however, required Soviet help. The June 1948 Berlin blockade persuaded the Senate to pass the Vandenberg Resolution, enabling the United States to make a commitment to Western European security (Smith 1991, 68). The Democratic Party's assumption of control of Congress after the 1948 elections also facilitated President Truman's efforts to commit the United States to the defense of Europe.

As in the case of the Brussels Pact, however, disagreements quickly arose with respect to the military strategy and command structure of the transatlantic alliance.[17] France, as well as Belgium, pressed for short-

---

[15] As in the case of the Treaty of Dunkirk, however, the Brussels Pact did not actually effect military cooperation among its member states. At its inception, three of its five signatories were engaged in colonial wars in Southeast Asia, making even national defense problematic (Wiebes and Zeeman 1991, 157).

[16] Marshall did not extend the invitation to Paris, because of its continued equivocation about Germany, as well as because of well-founded concerns about Soviet infiltration of the French government (Nuti 1991, 255). As it turned out, the second secretary of the British embassy in Washington, Donald Maclean, who did participate in the early stages of the Washington talks, was also a Soviet agent (Ferrell 1991, 21).

[17] The Europeans wanted the United States to commit itself to respond automatically to the limits of its resources if an ally were attacked. However, this conflicted with the constitutional allocation of power to declare war, as well as with the imperatives of domestic politics. As a result, Article 5 of the NATO treaty affirms the commitment of each of its members to assist any other in case of attack, but it leaves to each nation the decision about the specifics of its response (Barié 1991, 33).

term U.S. military aid; Britain and the Netherlands preferred a genuine transatlantic security arrangement; and the United States sought a long-term plan that included a resolution of the issue of rearmament in Europe (Bagnato 1991, 100; Ferrell 1991, 158).[18]

In addition, Britain viewed itself, and to some extent Europe more generally, as equal partners in NATO. Because France feared that Britain would orient the alliance toward the Mediterranean, however, it preferred U.S. leadership. The Anglo-French conflict contributed to the U.S. assumption of the preeminent role in NATO, symbolized by the appointment of General Dwight D. Eisenhower as its first Supreme Commander.

It was not until the outbreak of the Korean War in June 1950, however, that a resolution of the military issues outstanding became pressing. The United States began to demand the rearmament of Germany, creating opposition within both Germany and France. Concerned about adverse Soviet and French reactions, West German Chancellor Konrad Adenauer sought to substitute British and U.S. troops for indigenous German forces stationed along its eastern border (May 1991, 65).

France proposed the creation of a European Defense Community (EDC), which would integrate into a multilateral force German and other European troops (May 1991, 65). The EDC never materialized, however. Germany demanded full equality in it, and Britain refused to guarantee German membership in the organization. The coup de grace came from within France, however: none of its political parties supported either German rearmament or the replacement of exclusively French armed forces with a multilateral force. In August 1954, the French Assembly voted down the EDC (May 1991, 72).

The EDC's failure made clear that no feasible European alternative to Germany's rearmament and its entry into NATO existed. Thus, in October 1954, the Paris Treaties admitted Germany into the Atlantic alliance, conditional on Bonn's pledge to forgo the use of force as an instrument of territorial change and on London's commitment to maintain substantial forces on the European continent.

Thus, it was not the unilateral imposition of U.S. preferences on its major-power allies that created NATO. Rather, the alliance reflected political preferences endogenous to Britain, France, and the United States,

---

[18] When France threatened to withdraw from the negotiations unless the United States responded to its requests, the United States agreed to equip three French divisions on German territory (Bagnato 1991).

as well as a series of bargains among them to secure their common interests in deterring Germany and the Soviet Union. Indeed, both Britain and France viewed NATO as a means to protect themselves against Germany and the U.S.S.R. simultaneously. The United States joined to prevent the reemergence of the continental instability that had spiraled into world wars twice in the twentieth century.

In the end, then, the answer to the question of "who pulled whom and how much" to establish NATO lies in the substantial, but not complete, overlap of interests of the major powers on both sides of the Atlantic (Petersen, cited in Varsori 1991, 21). The negotiations that established NATO did not allow any of the major powers to realize all of its goals but did allow each to realize its most important objective. The comment of an early Secretary General of NATO is apt: the alliance, he observed, served to "keep the Americans in, the Russians out, and the Germans down" (quoted in Dunbabin 1994, 383).

THE SINO-SOVIET ALLIANCE

As is well known, the signatories of the 1950 Sino-Soviet Treaty of Friendship, Alliance, and Mutual Assistance were somewhat reluctant parties to it, given the legacy of World War II. In 1941, for example, Mao had refused to commit forces to deter a Japanese attack against the Soviet Far East (Goncharov, Lewis, and Litai 1993, 8). At Yalta and after, Stalin had made clear his intentions to maintain the wartime status quo in Manchuria and to restore the privileges Russia had enjoyed, however briefly, in late-nineteenth-century China.

The interests of both countries in reaching an agreement, however, proved more compelling than did the legacy of the Second World War. Mao needed Russia to secure China's unification and its defense; Stalin wanted a buffer zone in Manchuria. The price China paid for the treaty, however, would fuel its enmity toward Moscow. In a secret protocol to the treaty, Mao agreed, for example, to restrict to Chinese and Soviet citizens the right to live in Manchuria and Xianjiang (Goncharov, Lewis, and Litai 1993, 121). Yet, the alliance also left the Soviets unsatisfied: neither the treaty nor any of its ancillary agreements protected Soviet interests against the emergence of Sino-American ties or of a Chinese Tito.

The Korean War, however, enabled the Soviet Union to accomplish both goals. According to recent studies, Kim Il Sung sought Soviet aid to unify Korea. In case the United States intervened, Stalin insisted that

Mao condone Kim's initiative. Mao had no choice: if he expressed any concern about U.S. intervention, he would undercut his plans to invade Taiwan. Because the ensuing confrontation between Chinese and U.S. forces froze Sino-American relations for the next two decades, the Korean War enabled the Soviets to obtain the objectives that had eluded them in the 1950 treaty.[19]

The war also, however, reinforced China's determination to reduce its dependence on Moscow, leading it to demand Soviet help to establish a nuclear weapons program. Prolonged negotiations produced the New Defense Technical Accord in 1956, when the Hungarian Revolution and the Polish insurgency enhanced China's value to the U.S.S.R. The nuclear impasse that followed, however, was a major factor contributing to the end of the Sino-Soviet alliance in 1961.[20]

In sum, a historical review of the years between 1870 and 1903 and of those between 1946 and 1961 suggests that alliances are a good proxy for interests. A close relationship indeed does seem to prevail between the existence of common and conflicting interests and the presence or absence of alliance ties between major powers. Thus, it seems reasonable to use alliances as a measure of interests.

MAJOR-POWER REGIME TYPES AND ALLIANCES ACROSS TIME

Consistent with conventional wisdom, the historical reviews in this chapter suggest that interest patterns between major powers vary with the international system. In the multipolar system examined here, major-power interests do seem to be relatively fluid; during the Cold War, interest patterns are much more rigid.

This cross-temporal variation in interest patterns suggests that a similar variation exists in relations between democratic and other states: that is, before 1914, the character of major-power interactions makes it difficult to distinguish democratic from other country dyads. After 1945, however, the Cold War produces a pattern of strong common interests among democratic states. Here I test whether the data conform to the patterns evident in the historical narratives.

---

[19] This account of the Korean War is based on Goncharov, Lewis, and Litai (1993, chap. 5).

[20] For a detailed account of the Sino-Soviet split, see Chang (1990); Dunbabin (1994, chap. 15).

The Sample

According to the Polity II data set, Britain and France are both democracies and major powers between 1870 and 1903. The United States is both democratic and a major power between 1898 and 1903. The other late-nineteenth-century major powers—that is, Austria-Hungary, Germany, Italy, Japan, and Russia—are autocracies. Between 1946 and 1961, Britain, France, the United States, and Germany are both major powers and democracies, while an autocracy exists in the U.S.S.R. Between 1946 and 1949, the civil war in China renders it an anocracy; after 1949, it is classified as an autocracy (Gurr 1990).

Data on alliances are drawn from the COW project. The latter classifies alliances into three types: ententes, nonaggression pacts, and defense pacts.[21] Ententes pledge their adherents to consult others in the event of war. A nonaggression pact obliges each of its signatories to remain neutral if a war breaks out that involves another signatory. Defense pacts require their members to assist each other in the event any is attacked.

As Fearon (1997) notes, the three alliance types are sometimes treated as ordinal variables that reflect the strength of common interests between or among allies. A state's adherence to a nonaggression pact, however, seems to signal its concern that another signatory might attack it in the event it became involved in a war with a third party (Fearon 1997, 86–87, n.37). Thus, its validity as a measure of common interests is problematic.

Among the three alliance types that Small and Singer code, defense pacts represent the strongest possible written commitment states can make to each other. Moreover, they exert the most powerful effects on the behavior of their signatories (Kim 1991, 672; Siverson and Starr 1991, 61).[22] In the analyses that follow, therefore, I analyze all alliances and defense pacts separately. When the results differ, I emphasize those that emerge from the defense-pact analyses.

---

[21] The Small and Singer data are from ICPSR Study Number 5602. Alan Sabrosky supplied more recent data directly.

[22] Some studies (e.g., Sabrosky 1980) find that less than one-third of signatories honor their alliance commitments. However, as Fearon (1997, 86) points out, Sabrosky's calculations do not take into account whether the specific terms of the alliance are met. Examining the period between 1815 and 1939, Holsti, Hopmann, and Sullivan (1973) find that when these terms are met, 88 percent of allies honor their commitments.

TABLE 5.1

Probability of Alliance by Polity Type, 1871–1903: Fraction of Dyad-Years in Alliance and Defense Pacts

| | Dyad type | | | |
	Democratic-democratic	Other	χ^2 statistic	p-value
Alliances	0.0000 [39]	0.3089 [492]	16.88	0.000
Defense pacts	0.0000 [39]	0.1626 [492]	7.47	0.006

Note: The χ^2 statistics are the Pearson statistics for tests of independence of polity type and the probability of alliances and defense pacts. The numbers in brackets are sample sizes.

Results

Table 5.1 reports the probability of major-power alliances and defense pacts by polity type for the 1871–1903 period. In other words, the table shows the fraction of years that alliances in general and defense pacts in particular joined members of democratic and other dyads between 1871 and 1903. The table also contains a Pearson χ^2 statistic for a test of independence of polity type and alliance rates. It shows that members of major-power democratic dyads are significantly less likely than are members of other country pairs to ally with each other (p-value < 0.0005). The alliance rate for members of democratic dyads is zero; the corresponding statistic for members of nondemocratic dyads is about 31 percent.

   The table also shows that the results of the defense-pact analysis do not differ qualitatively from those of the all-alliance analysis. Given that democratic states do not ally with each other at all during this period, they obviously do not join defense pacts with each other either. In about half of the dyad-years in which nondemocratic states ally with each other, their alliances take the form of defense pacts. The difference between the defense-pact rates for democracies and other states is statistically significant (p-value = 0.006). Because of the empty-margin problem that the lack of alliances between democracies creates, no probit analysis is possible.

   Next I test whether alliance patterns shift with the conclusion of the

TABLE 5.2

Probability of Alliance by Polity Type, 1904–1913: Fraction of Dyad-Years in Alliance and Defense Pacts

	Dyad type			
	Democratic-democratic	Other	χ^2 statistic	p-value
Alliances	0.3333 [30]	0.3786 [243]	0.2338	0.629
Defense pacts	0.0000 [30]	0.2016 [243]	7.3727	0.007

Note: The χ^2 statistics are the Pearson statistics for tests of independence of polity type and the probability of alliances and defense pacts. The numbers in brackets are sample sizes.

Entente Cordiale. Table 5.2 reports the probability of major-power alliances and defense pacts by polity type for the 1904–13 period. The table also contains a Pearson χ^2 statistic for a test of independence of polity type and alliance rates. The table displays evidence of a shift in interest patterns consistent with the bipolarization of the major-power subsystem: democracies are as likely to ally with each other as are nondemocracies between 1904 and 1914 (p-value = 0.629). Table 5.2 also shows, however, that defense pacts remain significantly more common between nondemocracies than between democracies during this same period (p-value = 0.007).

Table 5.3 reports the results of a multivariate probit analysis of alliances in the decade before the outbreak of World War I. It shows that no statistically significant difference exists between the alliance rate of members of major-power democratic dyads and that of members of other country pairs in the decade before 1914 (p-value = 0.513). Again, the lack of any defense pacts between members of democratic dyads precludes a probit analysis of them.

Table 5.4 is based on data from the early Cold War period. It presents the results of an analysis of the independence of polity type and alliances, as well as a Pearson χ^2 statistic for a test of independence between the two. As all major-power alliances in this period take the form of defense pacts, separate analyses of defense pacts are unnecessary. The table shows that the members of major-power democratic dyads are allied during almost 90 percent of the dyad-years in the sample. The corresponding sta-

85

TABLE 5.3

Probit Analysis of Probability of Major-Power
Alliance, 1904–1913

Variable	Alliances
Constant	−0.1976**
	(0.0461)
Democratic	−0.0603
	(0.0922)
Contiguous	0.1327*
	(0.0605)
Log L	−177.90
Sample size	273

Note: The numbers in parentheses are standard errors, corrected for arbitrary heteroscedacity using Huber's formula. The coefficients are normalized to represent the derivative of the probability of the outcome with respect to a change in the explanatory variable. This is computed as $\beta\phi(\overline{X}\beta)$ where β is the vector of estimated parameters of the probit model, $\overline{X}$ is the vector of means of the explanatory variables, and ϕ is the standard normal probability density function. The sample mean alliance rate is 0.3736. *p < 0.05, two-tailed test. **p < 0.01, two-tailed test.

TABLE 5.4

Probability of Major-Power Alliance by Polity Type, 1946–1961: Fraction of
Dyad-Years in Alliance (Defense Pacts)

	Dyad type			
	Democratic-democratic	Other	χ^2 statistic	p-value
Alliances	0.8986	0.1404	101.04	0.000
	[69]	[114]		

Note: The χ^2 statistics are Pearson statistics for tests of independence of polity type and the probability of alliances for each period. The numbers in brackets are sample sizes.

TABLE 5.5
Probit Analysis of Probability of Major-Power
Alliance (Defense Pacts), 1946–1961

Variable	Alliance
Constant	−0.4804**
	(0.0579)
Democratic	0.8946**
	(0.1026)
Contiguous	−0.1219
	(0.0891)
Log L	−68.07
Sample size	183

Note: The numbers in parentheses are standard errors, corrected for arbitrary heteroscedacity using Huber's formula. The coefficients are normalized to represent the derivative of the probability of the outcome with respect to a change in the explanatory variable. This is computed as $\beta\phi(\overline{X}\beta)$ where β is the vector of estimated parameters of the probit model, $\overline{X}$ is the vector of means of the explanatory variables, and ϕ is the standard normal probability density function. The sample mean alliance rate is 0.4262. *p < 0.05, two-tailed test. **p < 0.01, two-tailed test.

tistic for nondemocratic dyads is 14 percent. As the table shows, this difference is statistically significant (p-value < 0.0005).

The results of probit analyses of major-power alliances by contiguity and polity type in the immediate postwar period are consistent with the results of the bivariate analyses in table 5.4. Table 5.5 shows that democratic states ally with each other at a significantly higher rate during this period than do members of other country pairs (p-value < 0.0005 for both). The effect of joint democracy is to raise the probability of an alliance by about 89 percentage points, relative to the rate for non-democracies.

Thus, the findings of these analyses are consistent with the patterns that emerge from the historical narratives. Conventional wisdom does indeed seem to capture important changes in interest patterns between pairs of democratic states and other major-power pairs across the centuries, as well as during the years approaching World War I.

Conclusion

The historical reviews in this chapter suggest that alliances are a good proxy for common interests. They also suggest that the interest patterns of democratic and other major powers changed radically across centuries, as well as during the latter part of the nineteenth and early twentieth centuries. Empirical analyses of alliance patterns support this interpretation. Together, the historical and empirical analyses suggest that it is feasible to test an interest-based explanation of cross-temporal variation in relative dyadic dispute rates for all countries, using alliances as a proxy variable. This is the subject of the next chapter.

Appendix 5.A

List of Major-Power Alliance Dyads, 1870–1903

Austria-Hungary-Britain, 1887–95
Britain-Italy, 1887–95
France-Italy, 1900–03
France-Russia, 1891–1903
Austria-Hungary-Germany, 1871–1903
Germany-Italy, 1882–1903
Germany-Russia, 1871–78, 1881–90
Austria-Hungary-Italy, 1882–1903
Austria-Hungary-Russia, 1871–78, 1881–87, 1898–1903

Appendix 5.B

List of Major-Power Alliance Dyads, 1946–1961

Britain-Soviet Union, 1946–47
France-Soviet Union, 1946–47
Britain-France, 1947-NA
Britain-United States, 1949–61
France-United States, 1949–61
China-Soviet Union, 1950–61

Explaining Relative Dispute-Rate Patterns

THE ANALYSES in chapter 4 showed that violent disputes do not occur at a consistently lower rate between democracies than between other states. More specifically, they showed that neither the incidence of wars nor that of lower-level disputes differs across country pairs before World War I. Between the wars, the evidence is mixed: war rates do not differ by dyad types, but democratic states are less likely than are other states to engage each other in lower-level MIDs. War and dispute rates between democratic states are significantly lower than are those between nondemocracies only during the Cold War.

In this chapter I examine whether these findings are consistent with an interest-based explanation derived from realist theory. For reasons explained in the last chapter, I use alliances as a proxy for interests. I find that the incidence of common interests between democratic states is lower than it is between other states before 1914. During the interwar period, the incidence of alliances is lower between members of democratic dyads than between members of other country pairs. After World War II, however, democratic states are much more likely than are other states to ally with each other.[1]

I also examine dispute-rate and interest patterns between 1816 and 1903. Both the last chapter and many much more comprehensive studies show that major-power interests and alliances became "bipolarized" in the wake of the Entente Cordiale. Because the dominant role of major powers in the system suggests that a comparable shift in interest patterns may characterize interactions in general, I analyze all country pairs between 1816 and 1903. I find that democracies engage each other in disputes at a significantly higher rate than do nondemocracies in this period. I also find that the incidence of common interests, as measured by alliances, is significantly lower between members of democratic dyads than between other dyad members in the years prior to the formation of the Anglo-French entente.

Thus, the analyses in this chapter suggest that common and conflicting

---

[1] Gartzke also finds that common interests among democracies play a significant role in explaining their relatively lower dispute rate between 1950 and 1985 (1998, 20).

interests provide a more compelling explanation of relative dyadic dispute rates than do common polities. However, because an interest-based explanation is not the only potential alternative to a polity-based explanation, I also examine an argument that Maoz and Russett (1993), among others, advance. In this argument, the maturation of democratic polities explains cross-temporal variation in dispute rates.

DISPUTE RATES, ALLIANCES, AND INTERESTS

From 1816 to World War I

Table 6.1 reports the probability of alliances and defense pacts by polity type for the pre-1914 period. The table also contains Pearson χ^2 statistics for tests of independence of polity type and the probability of alliance and defense pacts. As the results in the table show, no statistically significant difference exists between the propensity of democratic and nondemocratic states to ally with each other (p-value = 0.913). Democratic states, however, are significantly less likely to join defense pacts with each other (p-value < 0.0005).

Table 6.2 reports the results of a multivariate probit analysis of alliances and defense pacts, controlling for major-power status and contiguity, along with polity type. The effects of contiguity and major powers are

TABLE 6.1

Probability of Alliance Polity Type, 1816–1913: Fraction of Dyad-Years in Alliance and Defense Pacts

	Polity type			
	Democratic-democratic	Other	χ^2 statistic	p-value
Alliances	0.0264 [1475]	0.0260 [53996]	0.0121	0.913
Defense pacts	0.0020 [1475]	0.0225 [53996]	28.056	0.000

Note: The χ^2 statistics are the Pearson statistics for tests of independence of the polity type and the probability of alliances and defense pacts for each period. The numbers in brackets are sample sizes.

RELATIVE DISPUTE-RATE PATTERNS

TABLE 6.2

Probit Analysis of Probability of Alliance and Defense Pacts,
1816–1913

Variable	All alliances	Defense pacts
Constant	−0.0742**	−0.0675**
	(0.0023)	(0.0023)
Democratic	−0.0099**	−0.0354**
	(0.0025)	(0.0054)
Contiguous	0.0280**	0.0252**
	(0.0011)	(0.0010)
1 Major power	0.0120**	0.0102**
	(0.0009)	(0.0008)
2 Major powers	0.0421**	0.0286
	(0.0018)	(0.0016)
Log L	−4970.7	−4626.8
Sample Size	55441	55441

Note: The numbers in parentheses are standard errors, corrected for arbitrary heteroscedacity using Huber's formula. The coefficients are normalized to represent the derivative of the probability of the outcome with respect to a change in the explanatory variable. This is computed as $\beta\phi(\overline{X}\beta)$ where β is the vector of estimated parameters of the probit model, $\overline{X}$ is the vector of means of the explanatory variables, and ϕ is the standard normal probability density function. The sample mean alliance rate is 0.0260; the sample mean defense-pact rate is 0.0220. *p-value < 0.05, two-tailed test. **p-value < 0.01, two-tailed test.

positive and statistically significant in both cases. In the multivariate analysis, as table 6.2 shows, the incidence of alliances, as well as that of defense pacts, is significantly lower between democracies than between other states before 1914 (p-value < 0.0005 in both cases).

As before, it is interesting to note the absolute magnitude of the effect of the democracy variable on the propensity to join a defense pact. All else equal, before World War I, joint democracy reduces the probability that an alliance will form by about 1 percentage point and that a defense pact will form by about 3.5 percentage points. Given that the mean alli-

TABLE 6.3

Probability of Alliance by Polity Type, 1919–1939: Fraction of Dyad-Years in Alliance and Defense Pacts

	Polity type			
	Democratic-democratic	Other	χ^2 statistic	p-value
Alliances	0.0128 [5919]	0.0312 [31494]	61.147	0.000
Defense pacts	0.0086 [5919]	0.0057 [31494]	7.198	0.007

Note: The χ^2 statistics are the Pearson statistics for tests of independence of the polity type and the probability of alliances and defense pacts for each period. The numbers in brackets are sample sizes.

ance rate is 2.6 percent and the mean defense pact rate is 2.2 percent, these decreases are substantial.

The Interwar Years

Between the wars, a different pattern emerges. Table 6.3 presents the results of bivariate analyses of regime types and alliance probabilities. It also contains Pearson χ^2 statistics for tests of independence of polity type and the probability of alliance and defense pacts. As the table shows, democracies are significantly less likely than are other states to ally with each other (p-value < 0.0005). However, table 6.3 also shows that democratic states are significantly more likely to sign defense pacts with each other than are nondemocracies (p-value = 0.0007).

A multivariate probit analysis of alliances and defense pacts between the wars generates similar results. Table 6.4 shows that democratic states are significantly less likely to join alliances with each other than are nondemocracies in this period (p-value < 0.0005). They are no less likely to join defense pacts with each other, however, than are members of other dyads (p-value = 0.672). Contiguity and the presence of major powers exert positive and statistically significant effects in both cases, with one exception (i.e., in the defense-pact case, a dyad with two major powers).

Joint democracy exerts a substantial effect on alliance rates between the wars. It decreases the probability of alliance formation by 2.61 percentage

TABLE 6.4

Probit Analysis of Probability of Alliance and Defense Pacts, 1919–1939

Variable	All alliances	Defense pacts
Constant	−0.1035**	−0.0283**
	(0.0027)	(0.0021)
Democratic	−0.0261**	0.0003
	(0.0025)	(0.0006)
Contiguous	0.0474**	0.0103**
	(0.0019)	(0.0008)
1 Major power	0.0070**	0.0019**
	(0.0017)	(0.0006)
2 Major powers	0.0287**	−0.0004
	(0.0046)	(0.0019)
Log L	−4134.3	−1183.5
Sample size	37413	37413

Note: The numbers in parentheses are standard errors, corrected for arbitrary heteroscedacity using Huber's formula. The coefficients are normalized to represent the derivative of the probability of the outcome with respect to a change in the explanatory variable. This is computed as $\beta\phi(\overline{X}\beta)$ where β is the vector of estimated parameters of the probit model, $\overline{X}$ is the vector of means of the explanatory variables, and ϕ is the standard normal probability density function. The sample mean alliance rate is 0.0283; the mean defense-pact rate is 0.0061. *p-value < 0.05, two-tailed test. **p-value < 0.01, two-tailed test.

points, relative to the sample mean alliance rate of 2.83 percentage points. Contiguity exerts a strong effect, too, increasing the mean alliance rate by 4.74 percentage points.

The Cold War

After World War II, as the results of the bivariate analyses in table 6.5 show, democratic states are significantly more likely than are nondemocracies to join both alliances and defense pacts with each other (p-value < 0.0005 in both cases).

TABLE 6.5

Probability of Alliance by Polity Type, 1946–1980: Fraction of Dyad-Years in
Alliance and Defense Pacts

	Dyad Type			
	Democratic-democratci	Other	χ^2 statistic	p-value
Alliances	0.1326 [22498]	0.1081 [176335]	122.3	0.000
Defense pacts	0.1160 [22498]	0.0479 [176335]	1757.9	0.000

Note: The χ^2 statistics are the Pearson statistics for tests of independence of polity type
and the probability of alliances and defense pacts. The numbers in brackets are sample sizes.

As Table 6.6 shows, the same results emerge from a multivariate analysis. Alliances and defense pacts are significantly more common between
democratic states than between other states after 1945 (p-value <
0.0005 in each case). The incidence of defense pacts increases by about
4.1 percentage points if the members of a dyad are both democratic.
Relative to the sample average (i.e., 5.6 percent), this is an impressive
increase. Note also, however, that the other control variables exert even
stronger effects. All else equal, if a dyad contains two major powers, the
probability of a defense pact between its members increases by roughly
6.4 percentage points. If the members of a country pair are contiguous,
the corresponding increase is about 11 percentage points.

The results of this set of analyses suggest that the omitted interest variable
provides a better, albeit imperfect, explanation of relative dyadic dispute-rate
patterns across time than does the polity-based explanation. Before World
War I, as chapter 4 showed, neither war nor dispute rates differ across dyads.
In this same period, members of democratic country pairs are significantly
less likely than are nondemocracies to join either alliances in general or defense pacts in particular with each other. After 1945, dispute rates are lower,
and the incidence of common interests is higher between members of democratic dyads than between members of other country pairs.[2]

---

[2] Maoz compares the dispute rates of two sets of states: allied and nonallied nondemocracies, and allied nondemocracies and nonallied democracies (1997, 176). He finds that nonallied nondemocracies are less likely to fight each other than are their allied counterparts and
that allied nondemocracies are more likely to fight each other than are nonallied democracies.

TABLE 6.6
Probit Analysis of Probability of Alliance and Defense Pacts, 1946–1980

Variable	All alliances	Defense pacts
Constant	−0.2382**	−0.1757**
	(0.0006)	(0.0010)
Democratic	0.0141**	0.0405**
	(0.0021)	(0.0012)
Contiguous	0.2223**	0.1133**
	(0.0026)	(0.0016)
1 Major power	−0.0059**	0.0170**
	(0.0023)	(0.0014)
2 Major powers	0.0803**	0.0638**
	(0.0128)	(0.0068)
Log L	−65287.5	−38893.6
Sample size	198833	198333

Note: The numbers in parentheses are standard errors, corrected for arbitrary heteroscedacity using Huber's formula. The coefficients are normalized to represent the derivative of the probability of the outcome with respect to a change in the explanatory variable. This is computed as $\beta\phi(\overline{X}\beta)$ where β is the vector of estimated parameters of the probit model, $\overline{X}$ is the vector of means of the explanatory variables, and ϕ is the standard normal probability density function. The sample mean alliance rate is 0.1108; the mean defense-pact rate is 0.0556. *p-value < 0.05, two-tailed test. **p-value < 0.01, two-tailed test.

The evidence diverges most sharply from the argument between the wars. In this period, democratic states engage each other in significantly fewer disputes than do other states. Yet their alliance rate is significantly lower than that of other country pairs, and the incidence of defense pacts between them does not differ significantly from that of nondemocracies.[3]

As is true of many bivariate analyses, however, an omitted-variable problem plagues Maoz's results. Because contiguity is positively related to alliance formation and to disputes, the coefficient on the alliance variable is biased upward.

[3] See Siverson and McCarthy (1982) for a more detailed analysis of the interwar years.

TABLE 6.7

Probability of War and Lower-Level MIDs by Polity Type, 1816–1903:
Fraction of Dyad-Years in Conflict

	Polity type			
	Democratic-democratic	Other	χ^2 statistic	p-value
Wars	0.0010 [1049]	0.0015 [45186]	0.2232	0.637
Lower-level disputes	0.0230 [1044]	0.0073 [44804]	33.437	0.000

Note: The χ^2 statistics are the Pearson statistics for tests of independence of the polity type and the probability of wars and lower-level disputes for each period. The numbers in brackets are sample sizes.

From 1816 to the Entente Cordiale

Because a major shift in political interactions occurred in the decade preceding the outbreak of World War I, I examine this period separately here. Table 6.7 reports the results of bivariate analyses of polity type and dispute rates for all system members between 1816 and 1903. The table also contains Pearson χ^2 statistics for tests of independence of polity type and the probability of wars and lower-level disputes.

The results in the table show that war rates do not differ by polity type (p-value = 0.637). They also show, however, that members of democratic dyads are significantly more likely to engage in lower-level disputes with each other than are their nondemocratic counterparts (p-value < 0.005).[4]

The results of the multivariate probit analysis in table 6.8 display the same pattern. The table shows no variation in war rates across dyad types (p-value = 0.219). But it also shows that democracies are significantly more likely to engage each other in lower-level MIDs than are members of other country pairs before 1904 (p-value = 0.007).[5] The effects of

[4] If the sample includes both wars and lower-level disputes, democracies remain more likely to fight with each other than do nondemocracies but at a lower significance level (p-value < 0.08).

[5] A probit analysis that includes controls for peace spells of up to 30 years in length does not change the sign or significance of the coefficient on the joint-democracy variable. In a random-effects probit model, the sign of the coefficient on this variable remains the same,

TABLE 6.8
Probit Analysis of Probability of War and Lower-Level MIDs,
1816–1903

Variables	Wars	Lower-level MIDs
Constant	−0.0108**	−0.0366**
	(0.0014)	(0.0012)
Democratic	−0.0011	0.0033**
	(0.0010)	(0.0012)
Contiguous	0.0016**	0.0088**
	(0.0003)	(0.0007)
1 Major power	0.0010**	0.0040**
	(0.0003)	(0.0006)
2 Major powers	0.0013**	0.0088**
	(0.0006)	(0.0012)
Log L	−488.3	−1807.5
Sample size	46235	45848

Note: The numbers in parentheses are standard errors, corrected for arbitrary heteroscedacity using Huber's formula. The coefficients are normalized to represent the derivative of the probability of the outcome with respect to a change in the explanatory variable. This is computed as $\beta\phi(\overline{X}\beta)$ where β is the vector of estimated parameters of the probit model, $\overline{X}$ is the vector of means of the explanatory variables, and ϕ is the standard normal probability density function. The sample mean war rate is 0.0015; the sample mean rate for other disputes is 0.0076. *p-value < 0.05, two-tailed test. **p-value < 0.01, two-tailed test.

continguity and major powers are positive and significant in both the war and dispute-rate analyses.[6]

---

but it is statistically insignficant. This is the only instance in this book in which using either of these models produces a different dispute-rate result than does the standard probit model.

If wars and disputes are analyzed together, the coefficient on the joint-democracy variable is positive and marginally significant (p-value = 0.077).

[6] As noted in chapter 4, leaving alliances out of a model of wars and disputes resolves a simultaneity problem, at the expense of creating a potential omitted-variable problem. The dispute-rate analyses suggest that this is a particular problem for the pre-1904 period, be-

TABLE 6.9

Probability of Alliance by Polity Type, 1816–1903: Fraction of All Dyad-Years in Alliance

	Dyad type			
	Democratic-democratic	Other	χ^2 statistic	p-value
Alliances	0.0086 [1049]	0.0280 [45232]	14.44	0.000
Defense pacts	0.0000 [1049]	0.0248 [45232]	26.72	0.000

Note: The χ^2 statistics are the Pearson statistics for tests of independence of polity type and the probability of alliances for this period. The numbers in brackets are sample sizes.

Relative to the sample mean of 0.76 percentage points, joint democracy exerts a strong effect on dispute rates: it increases the probability of a lower-level dispute by 0.33 percentage points during this period.[7] As before, the other control variables exert still stronger effects: contiguity and a dyad with two major-power members each increase the probability of a dispute by 0.88 percentage points; the presence of one major power increases it by 0.04 percentage points.

Table 6.9 reports the results of bivariate analyses of polity type and alliance rates for all system members between 1816 and 1903. The table also contains Pearson χ^2 statistics for tests of independence of polity type and the probability of alliances and defense pacts. It shows that the incidence of alliances in general and defense pacts in particular is significantly lower between democratic states than between members of other country pairs during the pre-1904 period (p-value < 0.0005 for both).

Table 6.10 presents the results of a multivariate probit analysis of alliance rates for the 1816–1903 period. (An empty-margin problem pre-

cause the negative correlation between alliances and democracies may bias upwards the coefficient on the democracy variable. To check this, I included an alliance dummy as a regressor in the pre-1904 dispute-rate analysis. Doing so does not change the sign or significance of the democracy variable; the alliance variable is negative and statistically significant. Complete results are available from the author.

[7] To test whether these results are sensitive to the time period specified, I reran the analyses at two-year intervals between 1900 and 1906. In each case, democratic dyads are significantly more likely to become involved in lower-level MIDs. The effect ranges between 0.22 percent in the 1816–1906 analysis to 0.32 percent in the 1816–1900 analysis.

TABLE 6.10

Probit Analysis of Probability of Alliance, 1816–1903

Variables	Alliances
Constant	0.0783**
	(0.0026)
Democratic	−0.0287**
	(0.0047)
Contiguous	0.0313**
	(0.0012)
1 Major power	0.0119**
	(0.0010)
2 Major powers	0.0418**
	(0.0020)
Log L	−4407.1
Sample size	46281

Note: The numbers in parentheses are standard errors, corrected for arbitrary heteroscedacity using Huber's formula. The coefficients are normalized to represent the derivative of the probability of the outcome with respect to a change in the explanatory variable. This is computed as $\beta\phi(\overline{X}\beta)$ where β is the vector of estimated parameters of the probit model, $\overline{X}$ is the vector of means of the explanatory variables, and ϕ is the standard normal probability density function. The sample mean alliance rate is 0.0276. *p-value < 0.05, two-tailed test. **p-value < 0.01, two-tailed test.

cludes a probit analysis of defense pacts.) As in the bivariate analysis, the multivariate analysis shows that democracies are significantly less likely to ally with each other than are members of other dyads (p-value < 0.005).[8] The control variables remain positive and significant.[9]

[8] These results are also robust to changes in the time period analyzed. That is, the results do not change if the relevant period is defined as either pre-1900 or pre-1906. Complete results are available from the author.

[9] Analyses of the succeeding decade confirm that a change in patterns of preferences and interactions occurred in the years immediately preceding World War I. A multivariate probit analysis shows that no statistically significant difference obtains between the war rates of

The average incidence of alliances in this period is about 2.8 percentage points. The incidence drops roughly to zero if the prospective allies are both democracies. The presence of a dyad with two major powers or contiguous members more than doubles the alliance rate; the effect of one major-power member is to increase it by about one-third.

In sum, analyzing the century before World War I in a way that corresponds more closely to the historical evolution of the system provides compelling evidence against the democratic-peace hypothesis. The incidence of lower-level militarized disputes between democratic polities is actually significantly higher than is that between members of other dyads during the years between 1816 and 1903.

In addition, an analysis of alliance patterns during the pre-1904 period provides further support for an interest-based interpretation of variations in relative dyadic dispute rates across time. The incidence of alliances is significantly lower between democracies than between nondemocracies during these years. For both the pre-1904 and post-1945 periods, which account for 125 of the 165 years in the sample, then, the evidence is completely consistent with an interest-based explanation of dispute-rate patterns.[10]

AN ALTERNATIVE EXPLANATION

The evidence presented in this chapter and in chapter 4 is not consistent with the democratic-peace hypothesis. It suggests that an interest-based explanation provides a better fit to the data than does a polity-based explanation. Nonetheless, it is, of course, possible that other explanations exist that are also consistent with the evidence about dispute rates and alliance patterns presented in this book.

Among the candidates is an explanation that emphasizes differences among democratic polities themselves. Some observers argue that these polities vary both cross-sectionally and longitudinally in the extent to which they conform to a "deeply democratic" profile, that is, to the pattern of attributes that characterizes highly developed democracies.[11] They

---

pairs of democratic and other dyads during this decade; members of democratic dyads are marginally less likely to engage each other in lower-level MIDs (p-value = 0.07). Complete results are available from the author.

[10] There are 89 years before 1905, 20 years between the wars, and 36 years after World War II.

[11] This argument does not rest on strong empirical evidence. Maoz and Russett, for ex-

maintain that this variation can generate different dispute-rate patterns among democratic dyads themselves: that is, the more closely both members of a dyad conform to a deeply democratic profile, the lower is the probability of disputes between them (e.g., Maoz and Russett 1993, 629). Thus, to the extent that democratization is a function of time, the deep-democracy explanation is also consistent with variation in relative dyadic dispute rates across time.

Two problems afflict this explanation, however. First, the results of a test of the deep democracy argument do not provide strong support for it. Second, the explanation itself modifies the democratic-peace hypothesis in a way that raises serious questions about the distinctiveness of democratic polities with respect to the use of force.

Deep Democracies and Disputes

To test the deep-democracy explanation, the sample of democratic states was divided between those states that receive the maximum possible score of 10 on Gurr's democracy scale and all others.[12] Deeply democratic dyads are those in which both states receive a 10 on the Gurr scale.

There is a continuous increase in the proportion of deeply democratic dyads over time. Before 1914, 9.49 percent of all democratic dyad years are in this category, that is, those that include the United States, Switzerland, Greece, and Norway. Between the wars, the corresponding statistic jumps to 33.05 percent, as the set of deep democracies expands to include Britain, France, and Canada, among others. After World War II, 46.30 percent of democratic dyad-years fall into this category as, for example, West Germany, Italy, and Austria become members of this subset of democratic polities.

An analysis of the probability of war by democratic-dyad type for each period, as well as Pearson χ^2 statistics for tests of independence between dyad types and the probability of war, reveals that no difference in war rates exists between deeply democratic and other democratic dyads in any time period.[13] An empty-margin problem precludes using a more

---

ample, point to the progressive expansion of the suffrage to support their argument about the effect of deep democracies on dyadic dispute rates (1993, 627). Yet they do not present any data to show that expansions of the franchise have shifted the distribution of voter preferences about the use of force.

[12] This analysis appears in Farber and Gowa (1997).

[13] Because the number of expected entries in each cell is less than one, a single-tailed Fisher's exact test was used.

TABLE 6.11

Probability of Lower-Level MIDs by Polity Type and Time-Period, Democratic Dyads: Fraction of Dyad-Years in Lower-Level MIDs

| | Polity type | | | p-value |
| | Deeply | Other | | Fisher's |
Time period	democratic	democratic	χ^2 statistic	exact*
Pre–World War I	0.0000	0.0195	2.79	0.072
(1817–1913)	[140]	[1330]		
Interwar	0.0010	0.0043	4.38	0.025
(1919–36)	[1946]	[3957]		
Post–World War II	0.0009	0.0027	8.05	0.003
(1946–76)	[8788]	[10414]		

Note: The sample consists only of dyad-years where both states are classified as democratic (at least six on the Gurr democracy scale). Dyad years are classified as deeply democratic when both states obtain a score of ten on the Gurr democracy scale. The χ^2 statistics are the Pearson statistics for tests of independence of polity type and the probability of lower-level MIDs for each period. The numbers in brackets are sample sizes. *The p-values from the Fisher's exact test are single-tailed.

fully specified model to test whether the war rates of deep democracies and those of other democratic dyads differ in any of the three periods.

Table 6.11 reports the results of a bivariate analysis of the independence of lower-level dispute rates and democratic-dyad types. Because the number of expected entries in each cell is less than one, a single-tailed Fisher's exact test was used. The table shows only a marginally significant difference in the posited direction between the dispute rates of deeply democratic and other democratic dyads before 1914 (p-value = 0.072). The incidence of disputes between members of deeply democratic dyads is significantly lower than is that of other democratic country pairs during the interwar years (p-value = 0.025), as well as after World War II (p-value = 0.003).

An empty-margin problem also precludes a multivariate analysis of whether differences exist in lower-level dispute rates before World War I. However, the results of previous analyses suggest that lack of contiguity and major-power status alone may explain the relative dearth of disputes between deep democracies before 1914.[14] After 1945, because deep de-

[14] The United States becomes a major power only in 1898.

mocracies and strong common interests are perfectly collinear, it is impossible to distinguish between the deep-democracy and interest-based explanations.

Thus, as in the test of the original democratic-peace hypothesis, the war and dispute rates of members of deeply democratic dyads are not consistently lower than are those of other democratic country pairs. No difference exists in the war rates of the two different dyad types before 1914, between the wars, or after World War II. Only a marginally significant difference exists between the lower-level dispute rates of deeply democratic and other democratic dyads before World War I. Between the wars and after World War II, significant differences do exist in the posited direction.

A Pandora's Box

The democratic-peace hypothesis is based upon a dichotomy between democratic and other polity types. The deep-democracy alternative, however, assumes that a continuum of democratic polities exists. In doing so, it opens a Pandora's box: if important differences exist among democracies, no a priori reason exists to believe that differences among nondemocracies are any less consequential.[15]

For example, relations between autocratic states may differ from those between members of other nondemocratic country pairs. It is common knowledge that a shared interest in the preservation of conservative regimes seems to have moderated disputes among Germany, Russia, and Austria-Hungary in the late nineteenth century. The logic that motivates a disaggregation of democratic polities, then, would seem just as applicable to other regime types.

This creates empirical problems for democratic-peace proponents, however. Table 6.12 reports the probability of war of democratic dyads, autocratic dyads, and other dyads before 1914, between the wars, and after 1945.[16] The table also contains Pearson χ^2 statistics for tests of independence of polity types and the probability of wars. The results show that no significant differences in the probability of war among the three

---

[15] Among these differences are, for example, "ideologies, class coalitions, economic systems and institutional arrangements, including Communism, Islamic socialism, one-party rule, military populism, traditional kingship, and right-wing dictatorships" (Remmer 1998, 33).

[16] That is, those that include any combination of states other than two democratic or two autocratic states.

TABLE 6.12

Probability of War by Polity Type and Time-Period: Fraction of Dyad-Years at War

Time period	Polity type			χ² statistic	p-value
	Democratic-democratic	Autocratic-autocratic	Other		
Pre–World War I	0.0070	0.0016	0.0015	0.8869	0.642
(1816–1913)	[1475]	[1533]	[38552]		
Interwar	0.0000	0.0008	0.0003	5.1133	0.078
(1919–38)	[5919]	[3985]	[27498]		
Post–World War II	0.0009	0.0020	0.0004	12.137	0.002
(1946–80)	[22498]	[48753]	[127450]		

Note: The χ^2 statistics are the Pearson statistics for tests of independence of the polity type and the probability of war for each period. The numbers in brackets are sample sizes.

dyad types exist, except during the Cold War. In this period, the war rate of democratic dyads is lower than that of either autocratic or other dyad types.

Table 6.13 reports the results of a probit analysis of war rates that distinguishes among democratic, autocratic, and other dyads by time period. The results show that no statistically significant difference exists between the war rates of autocratic and democratic dyads before World War I (p-value = 0.193). Nor does any significant difference exist between the war rate of autocratic dyads and that of the base group of other dyads before 1914 (p-value = 0.665).

Between 1919 and 1938, no wars occur between members of democratic country pairs or between those of noncontiguous dyads. As this creates an empty-margin problem, the model for this period does not control for either variable. Table 6.13 shows that no statistically significant difference exists between the war rates of autocratic dyads and that of the base group between the wars (p-value = 0.299).

After World War II, there are no wars between members of democratic dyads. Thus, the model does not control for these dyads. The results in table 6.13 show that autocratic dyads are significantly less likely to engage each other in wars than are members of the base group (p-value = 0.047). The controls for power status and contiguity tend to be positive and significant, except between the wars.

Table 6.14 reports the probability of lower-level disputes between

TABLE 6.13

Probit Analysis of Probability of War by Time Period: Democratic and Autocratic Dyads

Variable	Pre–1914	1919–38	Post–1945
Constant	− 0.0102**	− 0.0312**	0.0026**
	(0.0012)	(0.0079)	(0.0004)
Democratic	− 0.0014		
	(0.0010)		
Autocratic	− 0.0001	0.0028	− 0.00015**
	(0.0002)	(0.0027)	(0.00007)
Contiguous	0.0019**		0.0006**
	(0.0003)		(0.0001)
1 Major power	0.0006**	0.0017	0.0003**
	(0.0003)	(0.0025)	(0.0001)
2 Major powers	0.0007	0.0034	0.0006**
	(0.0005)	(0.0044)	(0.0002)
Log L	− 569.4	− 64.3	− 503.8
Sample size	55390	2497	176203

Note: The numbers in parentheses are standard errors, corrected for arbitrary hetero-scedacity using Huber's formula. The coefficients are normalized to represent the derivative of the probability of the outcome with respect to a change in the explanatory variable. This is computed as $\beta\phi(\overline{X}\beta)$ where β is the vector of estimated parameters of the probit model, $\overline{X}$ is the vector of means of the explanatory variables, and ϕ is the standard normal probability density function. The mean war rate is respectively 0.0015, 0.0040, and 0.0004 for each of the three successive periods. *p-value < 0.05, two-tailed test. **p-value < 0.01, two-tailed test.

members of democratic dyads, autocratic dyads, and other dyads before 1914, between the wars, and after 1945. The table also contains Pearson χ^2 statistics for tests of independence of polity type and the probability of war.

The table shows that democratic country pairs engage in lower-level MIDs with each other at a higher rate than do either members of autocratic dyads or of other country pairs before the war. The differences among the three are ststistically significant (p-value < 0.005). Between

TABLE 6.14

Probability of Lower-Level MIDs by Polity Type and Time-Period: Fraction of Dyad-Years in Lower-Level MIDs

	Polity type				
Time period	Democratic-democratic	Autocratic-autocratic	Other	χ^2 statistic	p-value
Pre–World War (1816–1913)	0.0177 [1470]	0.0055 [15182]	0.0083 [38320]	30.529	0.000
Interwar (1919–38)	0.0032 [5913]	0.0050 [3979]	0.0035 [27424]	2.650	0.266
Post–World War II (1946–80)	0.0017 [19198]	0.0029 [39042]	0.0034 [106103]	15.820	0.000

Note: The χ^2 statistics are the Pearson statistics for tests of independence of the polity type and the probability of lower-level MIDs for each period. The numbers in brackets are sample sizes.

the wars, no statistically significant differences prevail across dyad types. After World War II, the dispute rate for autocratic dyads lies between the dispute rates of democratic and other dyads, and the differences among the three dyad types are statistically significant (p-value < 0.0005).

Table 6.15 contains the results of a probit analysis of the lower level MID rates of democratic, autocratic, and other dyads for each period. Before World War I, autocracies are significantly less likely to engage each other in lower level disputes than are either democratic or other dyads (p-value < 0.0005 for both). Between the wars, the dispute rate of members of autocratic dyads and that of the base group do not differ significantly (p-value = 0.365); the dispute rate of democratic dyads is significantly lower than is that of either autocratic dyads (p-value = 0.006) or other country pairs (p-value = 0.009. After 1945, members of both autocratic and democratic dyads are significantly less likely to engage each other in disputes than are members of the base group (p-value < 0.0005 for democratic dyads; p-value = 0.003 for autocratic dyads). In this same period, the difference between democratic and autocratic dyads is also statistically significant (p-value < 0.005).[17]

[17] Consistent with dispute-rate patterns, the results of probit analyses show that the alliance rate of autocracies is significantly higher than that of other dyads both before 1914 (p-value < 0.0005) and after 1945 (p-value < 0.005). The results for the interwar period are

TABLE 6.15
Probit Analysis of Probability of Lower-Level MIDs by Time-Period:
Democratic and Autocratic Dyads

Variable	Pre–1914	1919–38	Post–1945
Constant	0.0339**	−0.0085**	0.0126**
	(0.0018)	(0.0012)	(0.0007)
Democratic	−0.0005	−0.0007**	−0.0020**
	(0.0011)	(0.0003)	(0.0003)
Autocratic	−0.0033**	0.0002	−0.0005**
	(0.0006)	(0.0003)	(0.0002)
Contiguous	0.0093**	0.0029**	−0.0051**
	(0.0006)	(0.0004)	(0.0003)
1 Major power	0.0038**	0.0013**	0.0015**
	(0.0006)	(0.0002)	(0.0002)
2 Major powers	0.0080**	0.0031**	0.0049**
	(0.0010)	(0.0006)	(0.0006)
Log L	−2164.1	−633.5	−2690.2
Sample size	54972	37316	164343

Note: The numbers in parentheses are standard errors, corrected for arbitrary hetero-scedacity using Huber's formula. The coefficients are normalized to represent the derivative of the probability of the outcome with respect to a change in the explanatory variable. This is computed as $\beta\phi(\overline{X}\beta)$, where β is the vector of estimated parameters of the probit model, $\overline{X}$ is the vector of means of the explanatory variables, and ϕ is the standard normal probability density function. The sample mean dispute rate for each period respectively is 0.0077, 0.0036, and 0.0031. *p-value <0.05, two-tailed test. **p-value < 0.01, two-tailed test.

Thus, substantial evidence of an autocratic peace across time exists.[18] As such, the emphasis sometimes accorded to highly developed democracies implicitly suggests that the democratic-peace hypothesis is based on a

inconsistent with the dispute-rate analysis. In this period, autocratic states ally with each other at a significantly higher rate than do other dyads, despite the fact that their dispute rate does not differ significantly from that of the base group. Complete results are available from the author.

[18] The results of an analysis with temporal dummies are the same as those reported in the text. The results of an analysis of a random-effects probit model differ for the post-1945 period: the joint-autocracy effect is not statistically significant.

somewhat arbitrary distinction between polity types. On the basis of the empirical evidence alone, it seem to make as much sense to differentiate between autocratic and other dyads as to distinguish between democratic and other country pairs.[19]

CONCLUSION

The evidence presented in this and the preceding chapters is not consistent with a polity-based explanation. An alternative explanation based on the disaggregation of democratic polities does not receive strong support from the data. Nevertheless, it is certainly possible that other changes have occurred in the characteristics of democratic polities across time that may explain the variation in relative dispute rates between the pre–World War I and post–World War II periods. Neither these changes nor their theoretical foundations are readily apparent, however.

It is important to note here, too, that the evidence does not support the claim of those who argue that a democratic peace exists because these polities are "natural" allies. Thomas Risse-Kappen suggests, for example, that "liberal democracies are likely to form 'pacific federations' (Immanuel Kant) or 'pluralistic security communities' (Karl W. Deutsch)" (1996, 358). If this were true, the common-interest argument would simply reduce to the common-polity argument. However, the analyses in this and the preceding chapters show that the relative incidence of alliances between democratic states varies across time. Thus, the democratic-peace and the realist explanations cannot be reconciled on the basis of a "natural" ally argument.

Of the alternatives considered, then, a conventional realist explanation seems to conform most closely to the data. That is, the existence of common and conflicting interests, rather than common polities, seems to explain the propensity of members of country pairs to engage each other in armed conflict.

[19] Thompson and Tucker (1997, 431) analyze the pre-1914 and post-1945 periods. They disaggregate dyads into four types—democratic, autocratic, anocratic, and mixed—and use a lag structure. Their results differ from those reported above.

Conclusion

THE APPEAL of the democratic-peace hypothesis to U.S. decision makers is not hard to understand. As in the case of earlier efforts to export democracy to Latin America, it allows them to pursue a foreign-policy strategy that responds to "the powerful grip of liberal tradition" on U.S. beliefs about political and economic development (Packenham 1973, 20). Its appeal is further enhanced by the results of a series of empirical studies of the democratic peace.

The abrupt demise of the Cold War and the dissolution of the former Soviet bloc reinforced the attraction of this literature to policy makers. As critics of the Clinton administration were quick to point out, the end of the East-West split left U.S. decision makers without a foreign-policy rudder. Thus, the democratic-peace literature filled a void in Washington. Indeed, when the Clinton administration adopted a strategy of enlargement, its explanation for doing so seemed to be a textbook case of arbitrage between the ivory tower and the real world. Promoting democracy abroad, the administration observed,

> does more than foster our ideals. It advances our interests because we know that the larger the pool of democracies, the better off we, and the entire community of nations, will be. Democracies create free markets that . . . make for far more reliable trading partners and are far less likely to wage war on one another. While democracy will not soon take hold everywhere, it is in our interest to do all that we can to enlarge the community of free and open societies. (Clinton 1996, 2).[1]

---

[1] In this, as in many other cases, it is possible that the strategy of enlargement is largely rhetorical. Yet, in pursuit of democratization abroad, the Clinton administration has given both economic aid and technical assistance to Central and Eastern Europe, as well as to successor states of the U.S.S.R. It has also supported the expansion of NATO to include former members of the now defunct WTO.

It is, of course, possible to interpret the extension of aid to former Soviet bloc members as a means of advancing U.S. interests rather than, or in addition to, helping to establish democracy in these states. After all, the United States has a long tradition of supplying economic assistance to many countries, irrespective of their regime type, to induce them to follow its lead in world politics. Thus, U.S. aid to former members of the Communist bloc

In this book, however, I argue that it is a mistake to base foreign policy on the idea that a democratic peace exists. Neither its theoretical nor its empirical foundations are secure. The idea rests upon three allegedly distinctive attributes of democracies: a norm mandating peaceful resolution of conflicts, low trade barriers; and an institutionalized system of checks and balances.

Yet, as I argued in chapter 2, it is not obvious that a clear distinction exists between a norm of and an interest in peaceful methods of conflict resolution. The power attributed to the norm regulating dispute settlement may be attributable to interests instead: within, as between, states, the cost of resolving disputes peacefully is lower than that of its alternative. Moreover, it is not obvious why only democratic states would prefer a negotiated settlement to the use of armed force.

Proponents of the democratic peace also contend that higher trade volumes make democratic states less likely than nondemocracies to engage in violent disputes with each other. Irrespective of any other problems that afflict it, this argument can be sustained only if the intensity of conflicts of interests that occur between democratic states is no higher on average than that which divides nondemocracies from each other. Otherwise, the value of the interests at stake between democracies would exceed that between nondemocracies, canceling out the effects of the higher opportunity costs associated with the disruption of the allegedly higher trade flows between them.

Even assuming a control for conflict intensity, however, higher trade volumes will deter conflicts only under much more restrictive conditions than the democratic-peace literature assumes. As in the case of economic sanctions in general, the existence of competitive markets lowers the costs incident upon the trade disruption that can accompany conflict. Even when markets are imperfect, trade may not exert strong deterrent

---

could be a product of this tradition rather than a signal of a genuine U.S. commitment to enlargement.

Albeit not impossible, it is more difficult to interpret the Clinton administration's support for NATO expansion as an extension of traditional U.S. security interests rather than as evidence of a commitment to the construction of democratic regimes in Central and Eastern Europe. The United States will help to fund the effort to bring the military forces of Poland, Hungary, and the Czech Republic into conformity with NATO standards. Yet, the commitment of these countries to the Western alliance and their ability to avoid war remains uncertain. Thus, unlike the foreign-aid case, the extension of NATO's membership roster might place U.S. security interests at risk. This suggests that the commitment to a strategy of enlargement, while not irreversible, involves more than just cheap talk.

effects, as states trading in imperfect markets typically have incentives to continue to do so whether or not they are engaged in a dispute.

In other words, unless a conflict is so intense that trade is physically impossible, neither party to a dispute may have an incentive to disrupt the flow of goods and services between them. If one state had had a more profitable alternative to trading with another state able to exercise market power over its terms of trade, it would have exercised that option ex ante. More generally, the trade-related effects of even major wars arise primarily from the domestic reallocation of resources incident upon the prosecution of a war rather than from the deliberate trade disruptions states inflict upon each other (Milward 1979).

In any case, the trade-based explanation of the democratic peace makes sense only if democracies do, in fact, trade more with each other than they do with other states. However, existing studies do not provide consistent support for the proposition that trade varies as a function of dyadic regime type. Controlling for various economic and other political variables, these studies do not find that joint democracy exerts a positive and significant effect on bilateral trade flows (Gowa 1994; Gowa and Mansfield 1993).

The third argument that is advanced to support the existence of a democratic peace emphasizes the role of checks and balances. Yet, non-democracies may be able to constrain the ability of would-be renegade leaders to embark upon military adventures abroad about as effectively as democracies. That is, the crucial distinction across polities may lie in the form, rather than the effect, of the relevant constraints.

For example, some students of American politics believe that Congress abdicated responsibility for foreign policy to the president after World War II (see, e.g., Pastor 1976; Schlesinger 1974). In their view, although an independent legislature existed during this period, it was politically irrelevant. The results of the analyses in chapter 3 suggest that this phenomenon existed with respect to the use of force abroad long before the onset of the Cold War.

This may be attributed to the fact that involvements in militarized disputes typically do not produce the strong distributional effects characteristic of, for example, trade policy.[2] Because recourse to force abroad more closely resembles a public good, the political process that produces trade policy and that which generates security policy differ. The latter does not typically precipitate the same kind of political pressure on heads

---

[2] For an analysis of the trade policy process, see, e.g., O'Halloran (1994).

of states as do trade issues. Thus, political-market failures drive a wedge between the principle and practice of checks and balances with respect to the use of force abroad.

The empirical foundations of the democratic peace prove to be less robust than the sheer number of studies in the literature suggest. The analyses in chapter 4 conform in almost all respects to existing analyses. The one major exception is that the pre–World War I and the post–World War II worlds are examined separately. This approach was motivated by the fact that these two periods differ considerably from each other in ways that might be expected to have a strong effect upon dispute patterns (see, e.g., Mearsheimer 1990; Waltz 1979; cf. Hoffman 1990; Keohane 1990).

If the data are aggregated across the entire 1816–1980 period, the dominance of Cold War observations will obscure any variation that might exist between these periods. Thus, chapter 4 first analyzed the entire 1816–1980 period and then examined the pre–World War I and post–World War II periods separately. Splitting the sample generates findings that are inconsistent with the democratic-peace hypothesis. Before 1914, members of democratic dyads are just as likely to engage each other in wars and disputes as are members of other country pairs. Indeed, between 1816 and 1903, democracies are significantly more likely to engage each other in lower-level MIDs than are nondemocracies. It is only after 1945 that the evidence is consistent with the democratic-peace hypothesis.

The finding that relative dyadic dispute rates vary across time conforms to an interest-based explanation. Between the end of the Congress of Vienna in 1815 and the outbreak of World War I, several major powers dominated both the European continent and the international political system more generally. During most of this period, diplomatic relations between the great powers were relatively fluid. This pattern persisted until the first decade of the twentieth century, when, in response to the increasing German threat, the bipolarization of alliance blocs replaced it.

After World War II, the United States and the Soviet Union assumed dominance of what became essentially a bipolar world. The alliance that had united these states against the threat from Nazi Germany dissipated within two years of the end of World War II, as intractable conflicts of interest arose between them. Within a very short time, an East-West split emerged that would endure until the collapse of the Soviet Union in 1989.

A test of the interest-based explanation, using alliances as a proxy for common interests, yields results that are largely consistent with it. Democracies are less likely to ally with each other and are no more likely to engage each other in disputes than are members of other country pairs before 1914. They are less likely to ally with each other and more likely to enter armed disputes with each other before 1904. After 1945, however, they are more likely to engage each other in alliances and defense pacts and less likely to become involved in disputes with each other than are their counterparts in other dyads.

Thus, the most unambiguous and important message of this book is that the democratic peace is a Cold War phenomenon: that is, the available data show that the democratic peace is limited in time to the years between 1946 and 1980. A democratic peace does not exist in the pre-1914 world, and it cannot be extrapolated to the post-Cold War era. As a result, to the extent that U.S. foreign policy is based on spreading democracy abroad to enhance international stability, it rests upon very weak foundations.

A strategy of enlargement is also potentially explosive, for two reasons. First, recent work suggests that polities in transition to democracies are, in fact, much more war-prone than are states with intact political regimes. Democratizing states are also, surprisingly enough, somewhat more war-prone than are states that are becoming more autocratic (Mansfield and Snyder 1996a, 308; 1996b). That armed conflicts serve the interests of those that the advent of democracy threatens may explain the interaction between democratic transitions and international disputes (Mansfield and Snyder 1996a, 315–16).

Second, if the United States actively attempts to export democracy abroad, it seems destined to become embroiled in the intense struggles that prospective political change precipitates. While democracy might be welfare-enhancing for the society as a whole, politics is not about social welfare maximization, however defined; it is about distribution. Those who benefit from the political status quo will oppose democratization; those who stand to gain from change will support it.

Thus, if the United States assists prodemocratic forces abroad, it will gain not only new friends but also new enemies. To the extent that its support for indigenous prodemocratic forces is inadequate to precipitate significant political change, the United States will have to choose between abandoning them and intervening more forcefully on their behalf.[3]

---

[3] Layne argues that the logic of the democratic peace "inevitably pushes the United States to adopt an interventionist strategic posture." If democratic states are peaceful but

In the event, the U.S. decision seems to be a foregone conclusion. In the case of humanitarian missions in northern Iraq, Somalia, and elsewhere recently, the United States has withdrawn when political conflict transformed them into high-risk operations. Because fierce competition among groups for political control often creates the desperate conditions that elicit humanitarian responses, aid missions themselves often become embroiled in intense political struggles (Mandelbaum 1994). U.S. public opinion turns quickly against further involvement in these situations. There does not seem to be any reason to believe that interventions to support democratization abroad will generate a fundamentally different pattern of public support in the near future.

For these reasons, a strategy of enlargement seems ill-suited to U.S. interests in the 1990s and beyond. The democratic peace seems to be a by-product of a now extinct period in world politics. In addition, an enlargement strategy threatens to endanger rather than enhance U.S. security in the long run. It risks engaging the United States in foreign conflicts that it cannot resolve, and, as a result, it risks the ability of the United States to make credible commitments when it embarks on interventions abroad. This suggests that a more traditional strategy based on building common interests might make the United States better off than a foreign policy designed to construct democracies abroad.

---

others are "troublemakers," he argues, "the former will be truly secure only when the latter have been transformed into democracies, too" (1996, 198).

References

Albrecht-Carrié, René. 1973. *A Diplomatic History of Europe since the Congress of Vienna*. New York: Harper and Row.

Alesina, Alberto, and Howard Rosenthal. 1995. *Partisan Politics: Divided Government and the Economy*. Cambridge: Cambridge University Press.

Ashworth, Tony. 1980. *Trench Warfare 1914–1918: The Live and Let Live System*. London: Macmillan.

Axerod, Robert. 1984. *The Evolution of Cooperation*. New York: Basic.

Babst, Dean V. 1972. "A Force for Peace." *Industrial Research* 14:55–58.

Bagnato, Bruna. 1991. "France and the Origins of the Atlantic Pact." In *The Atlantic Pact Forty Years Later: A Historical Reappraisal*, edited by Ennio di Nolfo. Berlin: Walter de Gruyter.

Baldwin, David. 1980. "Interdependence and Power: A Conceptual Analysis." *Inernational Organization* 34, no. 4: 497–510.

———. 1985. *Economic Statecraft*. Princeton: Princeton University Press.

Balke, Nathan S., and Robert J. Gordon. 1989. "The Estimation of Prewar Gross National Product: Methodology and New Evidence." *Journal of Political Economy* 97, no. 1: 38–92.

Banks, A. S. 1971. *Cross-Polity Times-Series Data*. Cambridge, Mass.: MIT Press.

Barbieri, Katherine, and Jack S. Levy. 1998. "Sleeping with the Enemy. I: The Impact of War on Trade." Unpublished ms.

Barié, Ottavio. 1991. "The Final Stage of Negotiations: December 1948 to April 1949." In *The Atlantic Pact Forty Years Later: A Historical Reappraisal*, edited by Ennio di Nolfo. Berlin: Walter de Gruyter.

Bartlett, C. J. 1996. *Peace, War and the European Powers, 1814–1914*. London: Macmillan.

Baskir, Lawrence M. and William A. Strauss. 1977. *Reconciliation after Vietnam: A Program of Relief for Vietnam Era Draft and Military Offenders*. Notre Dame, IN: University of Notre Dame Press.

———. 1978. *Chance and Circumstance: The Draft, the War, and the Vietnam Generation*. New York: Alfred A. Knopf

Beck, Nathaniel, Jonathan N. Katz, and Richard Tucker. 1997. "The Analysis of Binary Time-Series-Cross-Section Data and/or the Democratic Peace." Paper delivered at the Annual Meeting of the Political Methodology Group, Columbus, Ohio.

Benoit, Kenneth. 1996. "Economic Interdependence: A Path to Peace or Source of Interstate Conflict?" *Journal of Peace Research* 33, no. 1: 29–49.

Blechman, Barry M., Stephen S. Kaplan, and David K. Hall. 1978. *Force without War: U.S. Armed Forces as a Political Instrument.* Washington: Brookings Institution.

Bohara, Alok, and William H. Kaempfer. 1991. "Testing the Endogeneity of Tariff Policy in the United States." *Economic Letter* 35: 311–15.

Bollen, Kenneth A. 1979. "Political Democracy and the Timing of Development." *American Sociological Review* 45, no. 4: 370–90.

———. 1983. "World System Position, Dependence and Democracy: The Cross-National Evidence." *American Sociological Review* 48, no. 4: 468–79.

Bollen, Keith, A., and Robert W. Jackman. 1985. "Political Democracy and the Size Distribution of Income." *American Sociological Review* 50, no. 4: 438–57.

Brace, P., and B. Hinckley. 1992. *Follow the Leader.* New York: Basic Books.

Bradley, John F. N. 1989. "War and Peace since 1945: A History of Soviet-Western Relations." *Social Science Monographs.* Distributed by Columbia University Press.

Brecher, Michael. 1993. *Crises in World Politics: Theory and Reality.* New York: Pergamon.

Brecher, Michael, and Jonathan Wilkenfeld. 1982. "Crises in World Politics." *World Politics* 34, no. 3: 380–417.

Brecher, Michael, Jonathan Wilkenfeld, and Patrick James. 1989. *Crisis, Conflict and Instability.* New York: Pergamon.

Bremer, Stuart. 1992a. "Are Democracies Less Likely to Join Wars?" Paper delivered at the Annual Meeting of the American Political Science Association, Chicago, Illinois.

———. 1992b. "Dangerous Dyads: Conditions Affecting the Likelihood of Interstate War, 1816–1965." *Journal of Conflict Resolution* 36, no. 2: 309–41.

———. 1993. "Democracy and Militarized Interstate Conflict, 1816–1965." *International Interactions* 18:231–49.

Bueno de Mesquita, Bruce. 1981. *The War Trap.* New Haven: Yale University Press.

———. 1990. "Big Wars, Little Wars: Avoiding Selection Bias." *International Interactions* 16, no. 3: 159–71.

Bueno de Mesquita, Bruce, and David Lalman. 1992. *War and Reason.* New Haven: Yale University Press.

Burkhart, Ross E., and Michael S. Lewis-Beck. 1994. "The Economic Development Thesis." *American Political Science Review* 88, no. 4: 903–10.

Callahan, Karen, J. and Simo Virtanen. 1993. "Revised Models of the 'Rally Phenomenon': The Case of the Carter Presidency." *Journal of Politics* 55, no. 3: 756–64.

Campbell, A. E. 1962. "The United States and the Old World." In *The New Cambridge Modern History. Vol. XI: Material Progress and World-Wide Problems, 1870–1898,* edited by F. H. Hinsley. Cambridge: Cambridge University Press.

116

Chan, Steve. 1984. "Mirror, Mirror on the Wall . . . Are the Freer Countries More Pacific?" *Journal of Conflict Resolution* 28, no. 4: 616–48.
———. 1993. "Democracy and War: Some Thoughts on Future Research Agenda." *International Interactions* 18, no. 3: 205–14.
———. 1997. "In Search of Democratic Peace: Problems and Promise." *Mershon International Studies Review* 41:59–91.
Chang, Gordon H. 1990. *Friends and Enemies: The United States, China, and the Soviet Union, 1948–1972.* Stanford: Stanford University Press.
Christensen, Thomas J., and Jack Snyder. 1990. "Chain Gangs and Passed Bucks: Predicting Alliance Patterns in Multipolarity." *International Organization*, 44, no. 2: 137–68.
Clinton, William. 1993. "Confronting the Challenges of a Broader World." U.S. Department of State, Bureau of Public Affairs. *Dispatch* 4, no. 39: 3.
———. 1996. *A National Security Strategy of Engagement and Enlargement.* Washington, D.C.: U.S. Government Printing Office.
Cohen, Benjamin J. 1974. "The Revolution in Atlantic Economic Relations: A Bargain Comes Unstuck." In *Crossing Frontiers: Explorations in International Political Economy*, edited by Benjamin J. Cohen. Boulder: Westview Press.
Cooper, Richard N. 1968. *The Economics of Interdependence: Economic Policy in the Atlantic Community.* New York: McGraw-Hill.
———. 1972. "Economic Interdependence and Foreign Policy in the Seventies." *World Politics* 24, no. 2: 159–81.
Cox, Gary W. 1990. "Centripetal and Centrifugal Incentives in Electoral Systems." *American Journal of Political Science* 34, no. 4: 903–35.
Crockatt, Richard. 1995. *The Fifty Years War: The United States and the Soviet Union, World Politics, 1941–1991.* London: Routledge.
Cronin, James E. 1996. *The World the Cold War Made: Order, Chaos, and the Return of History.* New York: Routledge.
Cuckierman, Alex, and Allan H. Meltzer. 1986. "A Positive Theory of Discretionary Policy, the Cost of Democratic Government and the Benefits of a Constitution." *Economic Inquiry* 24, no. 3: 367–88.
Curry, C. David. 1985. *Sunshine Patriots: Punishment and the Vietnam Offender.* Notre Dame, IN: University of Notre Dame Press.
Cusak, Thomas R., and Wolf-Deiter Eberwein. 1982. "Prelude to War: Incidence, Escalation, and Intervention." *International Interactions* 9, no. 1: 9–28.
De Leonardis, Massimo. 1991. "Defense or Liberation of Europe: The Strategies of the West against a Soviet Attack (1947–1950)." In *The Atlantic Pact Forty Years Later: A Historical Reappraisal*, edited by Ennio di Nolfo. Berlin: Walter de Gruyter.
de Senarclens, Pierre. 1995. *From Yalta to the Iron Curtain: The Great Powers and the Origins of the Cold War.* Oxford: Berg.
Dixit, Avinash. 1996. *The Making of Economic Policy: A Transaction-Cost Politics Perspective.* Cambridge, Mass: MIT Press.

117

Dixit, Avinash, and John Londregan. 1995. "Redistributive Politics and Economic Efficiency." *American Political Science Review* 89, no. 4: 856–66.

Dixon, William J. 1994. "Democracy and the Peaceful Settlement of International Conflict." *American Political Science Review* 88, no. 1: 14–32.

Downs, George W., and David M. Rocke. 1994. "Conflict, Agency, and Gambling for Resurrection: The Principal-Agent Problem Goes to War." *American Journal of Political Science* 38, no. 2: 362–80.

———. 1995. *Optimal Imperfection: Domestic Uncertainty and Institutions in International Relations.* Princeton: Princeton University Press.

Doyle, Michael W. 1983. "Kant, Liberal Legacies, and Foreign Affairs." *Philosophy and Public Affairs* 12, no.3 (summer): 205–35, and 12, no. 4 (fall): 323–53.

———. 1986. "Liberalism and World Politics." *American Political Science Review* 80, no. 4: 1151–69.

Dunbabin, J. P. D. 1994. *The Cold War: The Great Powers and Their Allies.* London: Longman.

Duncan, George T., and Randolph M. Siverson. 1982. "Flexibility of Alliance Partner Choice in a Multipolar System." *International Studies Quarterly* 26, no. 4: 511–38.

Edwards, George C., III. 1990. *Presidential Approval.* Baltimore: Johns Hopkins University Press.

Edwards, George C., III, and Tami Swenson. 1997. "Who Rallies: The Anatomy of a Rally Event." *Journal of Politics* 59, no. 1: 200–12.

Ekelund, Robert B., and Robert D. Tollison. 1981. *Mercantilism as a Rent-Seeking Society: Economic Regulation in Historical Perspective.* College Station: Texas A & M University Press.

Elster, Jon. 1989. *The Cement of Society: A Study of Social Order.* Cambridge: Cambridge University Press.

Fair, Ray C. 1978. "The Effect of Economic Events on Votes for President." *Review of Economics and Statistics* 60, no. 2: 159–73.

———. 1988. "The Effects of Economic Events on Votes for President: 1984 Update." *Political Behavior* 10, no. 2: 168–69.

———. 1996. "Econometrics and Presidential Elections." *Journal of Economic Perspectives* 10, no 3: 89–103.

Farber, Henry S., and Joanne Gowa. 1997. "Common Interests or Common Polities? Reinterpreting the Democratic Peace." *Journal of Politics* 59, no. 2: 393–417.

Fay, Sidney B. 1928. *Before Sarajevo: The Origins of the World War.* Vol. 1. 2d ed. New York: Free Press.

Fearon, James D. 1992. "Threats to Use Force: Costly Signals and Bargaining in International Crises." Ph.D. dissertation, University of California, Berkeley.

———. 1994. "Domestic Political Audiences and the Escalation of International Disputes." *American Political Science Review* 88, no. 3: 577–92.

———. 1997. "Signaling Foreign Policy Interests: Tying Hands versus Sinking Costs." *Journal of Conflict Resolution* 41, no. 1: 68–90.

118

Ferrell, Robert H. 1991. "The Formation of the Alliance, 1948–1949." In *American Historians and the Atlantic Alliance*, edited by Lawrence S. Kaplan. Kent, Ohio: Kent State University Press.

Ferris, Wayne H. 1973. *The Power Capabilities of Nation-States*. Lexington, Mass: Heath.

Fienberg, Stephen E. 1980. *The Analysis of Cross-classified Categorical Data*. Cambridge, Mass.: MIT Press.

Fiorina, Morris P. 1981. *Retrospective Voting in American National Elections*. New Haven: Yale University Press.

———. 1991. "Coalition Governments, Divided Governments, and Electoral Theory." *Governance: An International Journal of Policy and Administration* 4:236–49.

———. 1992. *Divided Government*. New York: Macmillan.

Fiorina, Morris P., and R. Noll. 1978. "Voters, Bureaucrats and Legislators: A Rational Choice Perspective on the Growth of Bureaucracy." *Journal of Public Economics* 9, no. 2: 239–54.

Fisher, Lewis. 1995. *Presidential War Power*. Lawrence: University Press of Kansas.

Gaddis, John Lewis. 1986. "The Long Peace: Elements of Stability in the Postwar International System." *International Security* 10, no. 4: 99–142.

Gartzke, Erik. 1998. "Kant We All Just Get Along? Opportunity, Willingness, and the Origins of the Democratic Peace." *American Journal of Political Science* 42, no. 1: 1–27.

Gasiorowski, Mark. 1986. "Economic Interdependence and International Conflict: Some Cross-national Evidence." *International Studies Quarterly* 30, no. 1: 23–38.

Gasiorowski, Mark, and Solomon W. Polachek. 1982. "Conflict and Interdependence: East-West Trade and Linkages in the Era of Detente." *Journal of Conflict Resolution* 26, no. 4: 709–29.

Gaubatz, Kurt Taylor. 1991. "Election Cycles and War." *Journal of Conflict Resolution* 35, no. 2: 212–44.

———. 1996. "Democratic States and Commitment in International Relations." *International Organization* 50, no. 1: 109–40.

———. 1997. "Elections and War: The Electoral Incentive in the Democratic Politics of War and Peace." Department of Political Science, Stanford University.

Geary, James W. 1991. *We Need Men: The Union Draft in the Civil War*. DeKalb: Northern Illinois University Press.

Gelpi, Christopher. 1997a. "Crime and Punishment: The Role of Norms in Crisis Bargaining." *American Political Science Review* 91, no. 2: 339–60.

———. 1997b. "Democratic Diversions: Government Structure and the Externalization of Domestic Conflict." *Journal of Conflict Resolution* 41, no. 2: 255–82.

Gilbert, Felix, with David Clay Large. 1991. *The End of the European Era, 1890 to the Present*. 4th ed. New York: W. W. Norton.

REFERENCES

Gilpin, Robert G. 1981. *War and Change in the International System*. Princeton: Princeton University Press.

Gochman, Charles S., and Zeev Maoz. 1984. "Militarized Interstate Disputes, 1816–1976." *Journal of Conflict Resolution* 28, no. 4: 585–616.

Goldstein, Judith. 1993. *Ideas, Interests, and American Trade Policy*. Ithaca: Cornell University Press.

Goncharov, Seiger N., John Wilson Lewis, and Xue Litai. 1993. *Uncertain Partners: Stalin, Mao, and the Korean War*. Stanford: Stanford University Press.

Gourevitch, Peter. 1986. *Politics in Hard Times: Comparative Responses to International Economic Crises*. Ithaca: Cornell University Press.

Gowa, Joanne. 1994. *Allies, Adversaries, and International Trade*. Princeton: Princeton University Press.

———. 1995. "Democratic States and International Disputes." *International Organization* 49, no. 3: 511–22.

———. 1998. "Politics at the Water's Edge: Parties, Voters, and the Use of Force Abroad." *International Organization* 52, no. 2: 307–24.

Gowa, Joanne, and Edward D. Mansfield. 1993. "Power Politics and International Trade." *American Political Science Review* 87, no. 3: 408–20.

Grossman, Gene M., and Elhanan Helpman. 1995. "The Politics of Free-Trade Agreements." *American Economic Review* 84, no. 4: 667–90.

Gurr, Ted Robert. 1974. "Persistence and Change in Political Systems, 1800–1971." *American Political Science Review* 68, no. 4: 1482–1504.

———. 1990. "Polity II: Political Structures and Regime Change, 1800–1986" (computer file). Boulder, Colo.: Center for Comparative Politics (producer). Ann Arbor: Inter-university Consortium for Political and Social Research (distributor).

Hansen, John Mark. 1990. "Taxation and the Political Economy of the Tariff." *International Organization* 44, no. 4: 527–51.

Hardin, R. 1982. *Collective Action*. Baltimore: Johns Hopkins University Press.

Hechter, Michael. 1987. *Principles of Group Solidarity*. Berkeley: University of California Press.

Hess, Gregory D., and Athanasios Orphanides. 1995. "War Politics: An Economic, Rational Voter Framework." *American Economic Review* 85, no. 4: 828–47.

Hewitt, J. Joseph, and Jonathan Wilkenfeld. 1996. "Democracies in International Crisis." *International Interactions* 22: 123–42.

Hoffman, Stanley. 1990. "Back to the Future, Part II: International Relations Theory and Post-Cold War Europe." *International Security* 15, no. 2: 191–92.

Hogan, Michael J. 1987. *The Marshall Plan: America, Britain, and the Reconstruction of Western Europe, 1947–52*. New York: Cambridge University Press.

Holsti, O. R., P. T. Hopmann, and J. D. Sullivan. 1973. *Unity and Disintregation in International Alliances*. New York: John Wiley.

Jacobson, G. 1993. "Congress: Unusual Year, Unusual Election." In *The Elections of 1992*, edited by Michael Nelson. Washington, D.C.: CQ Press.

James, P., and J. R. Oneal. 1991. "The Influence of Domestic and International Politics on the President's Use of Force." *Journal of Conflict Resolution* 35, no. 2: 307–22.

Jervis, Robert. 1978. "Cooperation under the Security Dilemma." *World Politics* 30, no. 2: 167–214.

Johnson, Harry G. 1953–54. "Optimum Tariffs and Retaliation." *Journal of Economic Studies* 21: 142–53.

Jones, Daniel M., Stuart A. Bremer, and J. David Singer. 1996. "Militarized Interstate Disputes, 1816–1992: Rationale, Coding Rules, and Empirical Patterns." *Conflict Management and Peace Science* 15, no. 2: 163–213.

Kaempfer, William H., and Anton D. Lowenberg. 1992. *International Economic Sanctions*. Boulder: Westview Press.

Katzenstein, Peter J. 1985. *Small States in World Markets: Industrial Policy in Europe*. Ithaca: Cornell University Press.

Kennedy, Paul M. 1980. *The Rise of the Anglo-Germany Antagonism, 1860–1914*. London: Allen & Unwin.

Keohane, Robert O. 1990. "Back to the Future, Part II: International Relations Theory and Post–Cold War Europe." *International Security* 15, no. 2: 191–94.

Kim, Chae-Han. 1991. "Third-Party Participation in Wars." *Journal of Conflict Resolution* 35, no. 4: 659–77.

King, Gary, Robert O. Keohane, and Sidney Verba. 1994. *Designing Social Inquiry: Scientific Inference in Qualitative Research*. Princeton: Princeton University Press.

Kydd, Andrew. 1997. "Game Theory and the Spiral Model." *World Politics* 49, no. 3: 371–400.

Lake, David A. 1992. "Powerful Pacifists: Democratic States and War." *American Political Science Review* 86, no. 1: 24–37.

Langer, William M. 1931. *European Alliances and Alignments, 1871–1889*. Westport, Conn.: Greenwood.

Langhorne, Richard. 1981. *The Collapse of the Concert of Europe: International Politics, 1890–1914*. New York: St. Martin's Press.

Layne, Christopher. 1993. "The Unipolar Illusion: Why New Great Powers Will Rise." *International Security* 17, no. 4: 5–51.

———. 1996. "Kant or Can't: The Myth of the Democratic Peace." In *Debating the Democratic Peace*, edited by Michael E. Brown et al. Cambridge: MIT Press.

Leeds, Brett., and David R. Davis. 1997. "Domestic Political Vulnerability and International Disputes." *Journal of Conflict Resolution* 41, no. 6: 814–34.

Levi, Margaret. 1997. *Consent, Dissent, and Patriotism*. Cambridge: Cambridge University Press.

REFERENCES

Levy, Jack S. 1983. *War in the Modern Great Power System, 1495–1975.* Lexington: University Press of Kentucky.

———. 1988. "Review Article: When Do Deterrent Threats Work?" *British Journal of Politics Science* 18, part 4: 485–512.

———. 1989. "The Causes of War: A Review of Theories and Evidence." In *Behavior Society, and National War*, vol. 1, edited by Philip E. Tetlock et al. New York: Oxford University Press.

Lewis, Paul G. 1994. *Central Europe since 1945.* London: Longman.

Li, Richard P. Y., and William R. Thompson. 1976. "The Stochastic Process of Alliance Formation Behavior." *American Journal of Political Science* 72, no. 4: 1288–1303.

Lian, Bradley, and John R. Oneal. 1993. "Presidents, the Use of Military Force, and Public Opinion." *Journal of Conflict Resolution* 37, no. 2: 277–300.

Lijphart, Arend. 1997. "Unequal Participation: Democracy's Unresolved Dilemma." *American Political Science Review* 91, no. 1: 1–14.

Lohmann, Susanne, and Sharyn O'Halloran. 1994. "Divided Government and U.S. Trade Policy: Theory and Evidence." *International Organization* 48, no. 4: 595–632.

Londregan, John B., and Keith T. Poole. 1996. "Does High Income Promote Democracy?" *World Politics* 49, no. 1: 1–30.

Lowe, John. 1994. *The Great Powers, Imperialism and the German Problem, 1865–1925.* New York: Routledge.

Lucas, R. E., Jr. 1972. "Expectations and the Neutrality of Money." *Journal of Economic Theory* 4, no. 2: 103–24.

MacKuen, Michael B. 1983. "Political Drama, Economic Conditions, and the Dynamics of Presidential Popularity." *American Journal of Political Science* 27, no. 2: 154–92.

Magee, Stephen P., William A. Brock, and Leslie Young. 1989. *Black Hole Tariffs and Endogenous Policy Theory: Political Economy in General Equilibrium.* New York: Cambridge University Press.

Mandelbaum, Michael. 1994. "The Reluctance to Intervene." *Foreign Policy* no. 95 (summer): 3–18.

Mansfield, Edward D. and Rachel Bronson. 1997. "Alliances, Preferential Trading Arrangements, and International Trade." *American Political Science Review* 91, no. 1: 94–107.

Mansfield, Edward D., and Jack Snyder. 1996a. "Democratization and the Danger of War." In *Debating the Democratic Peace*, edited by Michael E. Brown, Sean M. Lynn-Jones, and Steven E. Miller. Cambridge, Mass.: MIT Press.

———. 1996b. "A Reply to Thompson and Tucker." *Journal of Conflict Resolution*, 41, no. 3: 457–61.

Maoz, Zeev. 1997. "The Controversy over the Democratic Peace: Rearguard Action or Cracks in the Wall?" *International Security* 22, no. 1: 162–98.

Maoz, Zeev, and Nasrin Abdolali. 1989. "Polity Types and International Conflict." *Journal of Conflict Resolution* 33, no. 1: 3–35.

Maoz, Zeev, and Bruce Russett. 1993. "Normative and Structural Causes of Democratic Peace, 1946–1986." *American Political Science Review* 87, no. 3: 624–38.

Marra, Robin F., Charles W. Ostrom Jr., and Dennis M. Simon. 1990. "Foreign Policy and Presidential Popularity: Creating Windows of Opportunity in the Perpetual Election." *Journal of Conflict Resolution* 34, no. 4: 588–623.

Martin, Lisa. 1992. *Coercive Cooperation: Explaining Multilateral Economic Sanctions.* Princeton: Princeton University Press.

May, Ernest R. 1991. "The American Commitment to Germany, 1949–1955." In *American Historians and the Atlantic Alliance*, edited by Lawrence S. Kaplan. Kent, Ohio: Kent State University Press.

Mayhew, David. 1974. *Congress: The Electoral Connection.* New Haven: Yale University Press.

———. 1991. *Divided We Govern.* New Haven: Yale University Press.

McChesney, Fred S. 1997. *Money for Nothing: Politicians, Rent Extraction, and Political Extortion.* Cambridge, Mass.: Harvard University Press.

McCubbins, Matthew. 1991. "Party Governance and U.S. Budget Deficits: Divided Government and Fiscal Stalemate." In *Politics and Economics in the Eighties*, edited by A. Alesina and G. Carliner. Chicago: University of Chicago Press.

McGowan, Patrick J., and Robert M. Rood. 1975. "Alliance Behavior in Balance of Power Systems: Applying a Poisson Model to Nineteenth-Century Europe." *American Political Science Review* 69, no. 3: 859–70.

McKeown, Timothy James. 1984. "Firms and Tariff Regime Change: Explaining the Demand for Protection." *World Politics* 36, no. 2: 214–33.

Mearsheimer, John. 1990. "Back to the Future: Instability in Europe after the Cold War." *International Security* 15, no. 1: 5–56.

Merritt, Richard L., and Dina A. Zinnes. 1991. "Democracies and War." In *On Measuring Democracy: Its Consequences and Concomitants*, edited by Alex Inkeles. New Brunswick, N.J.: Transaction.

Midlarsky, Manus. 1988. *The Onset of World War.* Boston: Allen and Unwin.

Miller, Ross A. 1995. "Domestic Stuctures and the Diversionery Use of Force." *American Journal of Political Science* 39, no. 3: 769–85.

Milward, Alan S. 1979. *War, Economy and Society, 1939–1945.* Berkeley: University of California Press.

———. 1984. *The Reconstruction of Western Europe 1945–51.* Berkeley: University of California Press.

Morgan, T. Clifton. 1993. "Democracy and War: Reflections on the Literature." *International Interactions* 18, no. 3: 197–204.

Morgan, T. Clifton, and Kenneth N. Bickers. 1992. "Domestic Discontent and the External Use of Force." *Journal of Conflict Resolution* 36: 25–52.

Morgan, T. Clifton, and Sally Howard Campbell. 1991. "Domestic Structure, Decisional Constraints, and War: So Why Kant Democracies Fight?" *Journal of Conflict Resolution* 35, no. 2: 187–211.

Morgan, T. Clifton, and Valerie L. Schwebach. 1992. "Take Two Democracies and Call Me in the Morning: A Prescription for Peace?" *International Interactions* 17, no. 4: 305–20.

Moskos, Charles C. 1969. "The Negro and the Draft." In *Selective Service and American Society*, edited by Roger Little. New York: Russell Sage Foundation.

———. 1970. *The American Enlisted Man: The Rank and File in Today's Military*. New York: Russell Sage Foundation.

Mueller, John E. 1970. "Presidential Popularity from Truman to Johnson." *American Political Science Review* 64, no. 1: 18–34.

———. 1973. *War, Presidents and Public Opinion*. New York: John Wiley.

———. 1994. *Policy and Opinion in the Gulf War*. Chicago: University of Chicago Press.

North, Douglass C. 1981. *Structure and Change in Economic History*. New York: W. W. Norton.

Nuti, Leopoldo. 1991. "The Italian Military and the Atlantic Pact." In *The Atlantic Pact Forty Years Later: A Historical Reappraisal*, edited by Ennio di Nolfo. Berlin: Walter de Gruyter.

O'Halloran, Sharyn. 1994. *Politics, Process, and American Trade Policy*. Ann Arbor: University of Michigan Press.

Olson, Maucur. 1993. "Dictatorship, Democracy, and Development." *American Political Science Review* 87, no. 3: 567–76.

Oneal, John R., Brad Lian, and James H. Joyner Jr. 1996. "Are the American People 'Pretty Prudent'? Public Responses to U.S. Uses of Force, 1950–1988." *International Studies Quarterly* 40, no. 2: 261–79.

Oneal, John R., Francis H. Oneal, Zeev Maoz, and Bruce Russett. 1996. "The Liberal Peace: Interdependence, Democracy and International Conflict." *Journal of Peace Research* 33, no. 1: 11–29.

Oneal, John, and James Lee Ray. 1996. "New Tests of the Democratic Peace: Controlling for Economic Interdependence, 1950–1985." Paper presented at the Annual Meeting of the International Studies Association, San Diego, Calif.

Oneal, John R., and Bruce M. Russett. 1997. "The Classical Liberals Were Right: Democracy, Interdependence, and Conflict, 1950–1985." *International Studies Quarterly* 41, no. 2: 267–39.

Oren, Ido. 1995. "The Subjectivity of the 'Democratic' Peace: Changing U.S. Perceptions of Imperial Germany." *International Security* 20, no. 2: 147–84.

Ostrom, Charles W., and Dennis M. Simon. 1985. "Promise and Performance: A Dynamic Model of Presidential Popularity." *American Political Science Review* 79, no. 2: 334–58.

Ostrom, Charles W., Dennis M. Simon, and Brian L. Job. 1986. "The President and the Political Use of Force." *American Political Science Review* 80, no. 2: 541–66.

Owen, John A. 1994. "How Liberalism Produces Democratic Peace." *International Security* 19, no. 2: 87–125.

———. 1997. *Liberal Peace, Liberal War: American Politics and International Security.* Ithaca: Cornell University Press.

Oye, Kenneth A. 1985. "The Sterling-Dollar-Franc Triangle: Monetary Diplomacy 1929–1937." *World Politics* 38, no. 1: 173–99.

Packenham, Robert A. 1973. *Liberal America and the Third World: Political Development Ideas in Foreign Aid and Social Science.* Princeton: Princeton University Press.

Pastor, Robert A. 1976. *Congress and the Politics of U.S. Foreign Economic Policy, 1929–76.* Berkeley: University of California Press.

Persson, T., and G. Tabellini. 1990. *Macroeconomic Policy, Credibility, and Politics.* Chur, Switzerland: Harwood Academic Publishers.

Poivdeden, Raymond. 1991. "Ambiguous Partnership: France, the Marshall Plan, and the Problem of Germany." In *The Marshall Plan and Germany: Western German Development within the Framework of the European Recovery Program,* edited by Charles S. Maier. New York: Berg

Polachek, Simon W. 1980. "Conflict and Trade." *Journal of Conflict Resolution* 24: 55–78.

Poole, Keith T., and Howard Rosenthal. 1991. "Patterns of Congressional Voting." *American Journal of Political Science* 35, no. 1: 228–78.

Posen, Barry R. 1984. *The Sources of Military Doctrine: France, Britain, and Germany between the World Wars.* Ithaca: Cornell University Press.

Powell, Robert. 1990. *Nuclear Deterrence Theory: The Problem of Credibility.* Cambridge: Cambridge University Press.

———. 1996a. "Stability and the Distribution of Power." *World Politics* 48, no. 2: 239–67.

———. 1996b. "Uncertainty, Shifting Power, and Appeasement." *American Political Science Review* 90, no. 4: 749–64.

Prezeworski, Adam. 1991. *Democracy and the Market: Political and Economic Reforms in Eastern Europe and Latin America.* New York: Cambridge University Press.

Ray, James Lee. 1993. "Wars between Democracies: Rare or Nonexistent?" *International Interactions* 18, no. 3: 251–76.

———. 1995. *Democracy and International Conflict: An Evaluation of the Democratic Peace Proposition.* South Carolina: University of South Carolina Press.

Remmer, Karen L. 1998. "Does Democracy Promote Interstate Cooperation? Lessons from the Mercosur Region." *International Studies Quarterly* 42, no. 1: 25–51.

Risse-Kappen, Thomas. 1996. "Collective Identity in a Democratic Community:

The Case of NATO." In *The Culture of National Security*, edited by Peter J. Katzenstein. Ithaca: Cornell University Press.

Risse-Kappen, Thomas. 1995. *Cooperation Among Democracies: The European Influence on U.S. Foreign Policy*. Princeton: Princeton University Press.

Robinson, R. E. 1962. "The Partition in Africa." In *The New Cambridge Modern History. Vol II: Material Progress and World-Wide Problems 1870–1898*, edited by F. H. Hinsley. Cambridge: Cambridge University Press.

Rogoff, Kenneth. 1990. "Equilibrium Political Budget Cycles." *American Economic Review* 80, no. 1: 21–36.

Rogoff, Kenneth, and Anne Sibert. 1988. "Elections and Macroeconomic Policy Cycles." *Review of Economic Studies* 55:1–16.

Rogowski, Ronald. 1989. *Commerce and Coalitions*. Princeton: Princeton University.

Romer, Christina. 1989. "The Prewar Business Cycle Reconsidered: New Estimates of Gross National Product, 1869–1908." *Journal of Political Economy* 97, no. 1: 1–37.

Rosecrance, Richard. 1976. "Introduction." In *America as an Ordinary Country: U.S. Foreign Policy and the Future*, edited by Richard Rosecrance. Ithaca: Cornell University Press.

Rousseau, David L., Christopher Gelpi, Dan Reiter, and Paul K. Huth. 1996. "Assessing the Dyadic Nature of the Democratic Peace, 1918–88." *American Political Science Review* 90, no. 3: 512–33.

Rummell, R. J. 1968. "The Relationship between National Attributes and Foreign Conflict Behavior." In *Quantitative International Politics: Insights and Evidence*, edited by J. David Singer. Englewood Cliffs, N.J.: Prentice Hall.

Russett, Bruce M. 1990. *Controlling the Sword: The Democratic Governance of National Security*. Cambridge, Mass: Harvard University Press.

———. 1993. *Grasping the Democratic Peace: Principles for a Post–Cold War World*. Princeton: Princeton University Press.

———. 1995. "The Democratic Peace: 'And Yet It Moves,'" *International Security* 19, no. 4: 164–75.

Sabrosky, Alan N. 1980. "Interstate Alliances: Their Reliability and the Expansion of War." In *The Correlates of War II: Testing Some Realpolitik Models*, edited by J. David Singer. New York: Free Press.

Sargent T., and N. Wallace. 1975. "'Rational' Expectations, the Optimal Monetary Instrument and the Optimal Money Supply Rule." *Journal of Political Economy* 83, no. 2: 241–54.

Schattschneider, E. E. 1935 *Politics, Pressures and the Tariff*. Englewood Cliffs, N.J.: Prentice Hall.

Schlesinger, Arthur A. 1974. *The Imperial Presidency*. New York: Popular Library.

Schroeder, Paul W. 1976. "Alliances, 1915–1945: Weapons of Power and Tools of Management." In *Historical Dimensions of National Security Problems*, edited by Klaus Knorr. Lawrence: University of Kansas Press.

Schultz, Kenneth A. 1995. "The Politics of the Political Business Cycle." *British Journal of Political Science* 25, no. 1: 79–99.

———. forthcoming. "Domestic Opposition and Signaling in International Crises." *American Political Science Review.*

Schweller, Randall L. 1994. "Bandwagoning for Profit: Bringing the Revisionist State Back in." *International Security* 19, no. 1: 72–107.

Scott, John Finley. 1971. *Internationalization of Norms: A Sociological Theory of Moral Commitment.* Englewood Cliffs, N.J.: Prentice Hall.

Segal, David R. 1989. *Recruiting for Uncle Sam: Citizenship and Minority Manpower Policy.* Lawrence: University Press of Kansas.

Senese, Paul. 1997. "Between Dispute and War: The Effect of Joint Democracy on Interstate Conflict Escalation." *Journal of Politics* 59, no. 1: 1–27.

Siverson, Randolph M., and Juliann Emmons. 1991. "Birds of a Feather: Democratic Political Systems and Alliance Choices in the Twentieth Century." *Journal of Conflict Resolution* 35, no. 2: 285–306.

Siverson, Randolph M., and Charles McCarthy. 1982. "Alliances in the Interwar Era, 1919–1939: A Re-Examination." *Western Political Quarterly* 35: 24–32.

Siverson, Randolph M., and Harvey Starr. 1991. *The Diffusion of War: A Study of Opportunity and Willingness.* Ann Arbor: University of Michigan Press.

Small, Melvin, and J. David Singer. 1969. "Formal Alliances, 1816–1965: An Extension of the Basic Data." *Journal of Peace Research* 3, no. 1: 257–82.

———. 1976. "The War-Proneness of Democratic Regimes." *Jerusalem Journal of International Relations* 1, no. 1: 58–69.

———. 1982. *Resort to Arms: International and Civil Wars, 1816–1980.* Beverly Hills: Sage.

Smith, Alastair. 1996. "Diversionary Foreign Policy in Democratic Systems." *International Studies Quarterly* 40, no. 1: 133–53.

Smith, Gaddis. 1991. "The Atlantic Pact as a Problem of U.S. Diplomacy." In *The Atlantic Pact Forty Years Later: A Historical Reappraisal,* edited by Ennio di Nolfo. Berlin: Walter de Gruyter.

Snyder, Glenn H. 1984. "The Security Dilemma in Alliance Politics." *World Politics* 36, no. 4: 461–95.

———. 1997. *Alliance Politics,* Ithaca: Cornell University Press.

Spiro, David E. 1994. "The Insignificance of the Liberal Peace." *International Security* 19, no. 4: 50–86.

Stoll, Richard J. 1984. "The Guns of November: Presidents, Elections and the Use of Force, 1947–1982." *Journal of Conflict Resolution* 28, no. 2: 231–46.

Taylor, A. J. P. 1962. "International Relations." In *The New Cambridge Modern History, vol. II: Material Progress and World-Wide Problems, 1870–1898,* edited by F. H. Hinsley. Cambridge: Cambridge University Press.

Thompson, William R. 1985. "Cycles of General, Hegemonic, and Global War." In *Dynamic Models of International Conflict,* edited by Urs Luterbacher and Michael D. Ward. Boulder, Colo.: Lynne Rienner.

————. 1993. "The Size of War, Structural and Geopolitical Contexts, and Theory Building/Testing." *International Interactions* 18, no. 3: 183–200.

Thompson, William R., and Richard M. Tucker. 1997. "A Tale of Two Democratic Peace Critiques." *Journal of Conflict Resolution* 41, no. 3: 428–54.

Tullock, Gordon. 1987. *Autocracy*. Dordrecht: Kluwer.

Varsori, Antonio. 1991. "The First Stage of Negotiations: December 1947 to June 1948." In *The Atlantic Pact Forty Years Later: A Historical Reappraisal*, edited by Ennio di Nolfo. Berlin: Walter de Gruyter.

Vernon, Richard. 1971. *Sovereignty at Bay*. New York: Basic Books.

Walt, Stephen M. 1987. *The Origins of Alliances*. Ithaca: Cornell University Press.

Waltz, Kenneth N. 1954. *Man, the State and War: A Theoretical Analysis*. New York: Columbia University Press.

————. 1979. *Theory of International Politics*. Reading, Mass: Addison Wesley.

Weede, Erich. 1992. "Some Simple Calculations on Democracy and War Involvement." *Journal of Peace Research* 29, no. 4: 377–84.

Weingast, Barry R., Kenneth Shepsle, and Christopher Johnson. 1981. "The Political Economy of Benefits and Costs: A Neoclassical Approach to Distributive Politics." *Journal of Political Economy* 89, no. 4: 642–64.

Wesseling, H. L. 1996. *Divide and Rule: The Partition of Africa, 1880–1914*. Westport, Conn.: Praeger.

White, John Albert. 1995. *Transition to Global Rivalry: Alliance Diplomacy and the Quadruple Entente, 1895–1907*. New York: Cambridge University Press.

Wiebes, Cies, and Bern Zeeman. 1991. "The Origins of Western Defense, Belgian and Dutch Perspectives 1940–1949." In *The Atlantic Pact Forty Years Later: A Historical Reappraisal*, edited by Ennio di Nolfo. Berlin: Walter de Gruyter.

Yarbrough, Beth V., and Robert M. Yarbrough. 1992. *Cooperation and Governance in International Trade*. Princeton: Princeton University Press.

Index

Abdolali, Nasrin, 4, 5, 44
Adenauer, Konrad, 80
Aegean Sea, Russian interests in, 72
Albrecht-Carrié, René, 70
Alesina, Alberto, 33, 34
Alliances, 83, 84–88; Cold War and, 10; different forms of, 83; after Entente Cordiale, 85, 89–90; before Entente Cordiale, 84; interests and, 10, 52, 68–88; interwar period and, 92–93, 95; nature of, 70; polities and, 84–88; post–World War II, 76–82, 85–87, 93–95; pre–World War I, 10, 71–76, 84–85, 90–92; process of formation, 55; simultaneity problem of conflict and, 52–54; World War II and, 77–78
Allied Control Council, 77
Alsace Lorraine, French and German interests in, 75–76
Anglo-Japanese Treaty, 74
Anglo-Russian Entente, 75–76
Anocracies, Gurr definition of, 49–50, 50n
Ashworth, Tony, 22n
Asia: British and French interests in, 74; British and Russian interests in, 71, 73–74
Asymmetric information: bargaining and, 25–26; in international system, 69; political market failures and, 25–26
Austria, 101
Austria-Hungary, 71–76, 83, 103
Autocracies: alliances and, 84–88; conflict and, 104–106; conflicts compared to democracies, 104–106; Gurr definition of, 49–50; MIDs and, 105–106; war and, 104–105
Autocratic peace, empirical evidence for, 104–107
Axelrod, Robert, 25n

Babst, Dean V., 4
Bagnato, Bruna, 80, 80n

Baldwin, David, 14n, 16
Balkans, 72; German and Russian interests in, 71–73
Balke, Nathan, 29
Banks, A.S., 49n
Barbieri, Katherine, 16n
Bargaining: asymmetric information and, 25–26; conflict and, 13; signaling and, 13n
Barié, Ottavio, 78, 79n
Bartlett, C.J., 74
Baskir, Lawrence M., 22, 22n
Beck, Nathaniel, 17n, 57, 58
Belgium, 79, 80
Benelux countries, 79
Benoit, Kenneth, 5n
Berlin blockade, 77, 79
Bevin, Ernest, 78
Bickers, Kenneth N., 26
Bipolarity. See Post–World War II period
Bismarck, Otto von, 72
Blechman, Barry M., 30n
Bohara, Alok, 24n
Bollen, Keith A., 52
Brace, P., 34
Bradley, John F.N., 70
Brecher, Michael, 30n
Bremer, Stuart, 4, 5, 18n, 25, 30, 32, 32n, 35, 39, 40, 44, 48n, 49n, 51, 58n
Bretton Woods monetary system, 78n
Britain, 71, 73–77, 79, 80–81, 83, 101
Brock, William, 15
Bronson, Rachael, 8, 15
Brussels Treaty, 79, 79n
Bueno de Mesquita, Bruce, 5, 10, 19, 36, 52, 69
Bulgaria, 72
Bulgarian Crisis, 73
Burkhart, Ross E., 52, 52n

Callahan, Karen J., 26
Campbell, A.E., 70

129